# ECONOMIC GROWTH AND FOOD SECURITY

# ECONOMIC GROWTH AND FOOD SECURITY

*By*

**Dr. M. Lakshmi Narasaiah**
M.A., Ph.D.

*Professor of Economics*
*Co-ordinator, Dept. of M.B.A. and Commerce*
*Special Officer*
*Sri Krishnadevaraya University Post-graduate Centre*
*Kurnool–518 002*
*Andhra Pradesh*
*(India)*

**DISCOVERY PUBLISHING HOUSE PVT. LTD.**
**NEW DELHI-110 002**

First Published – 2008
Reprinted – 2025

ISBN: 978-81-8356-310-9



**Economic Growth and Food Security**

*Published by:*
**DISCOVERY PUBLISHING HOUSE PVT. LTD.**
4383/4B, Ansari Road, Darya Ganj
New Delhi-110 002 (India)
*Phone*: +91-11-23279245; 23253475; 43596065
*Mobile*: +91 9811179893 / +91 9871656464
*E-mail*: discoverybooksindia@gmail.com
orderdphbooks@gmail.com
namitwasan9@gmail.com
*web*: www.discoverypublishinggroup.com

*Printed at:*
Infinity Imaging Systems
Delhi

# Preface

Will there be enough food to feed 8 billion people who will live on earth in 25 years' time? Surprisingly few people, at least in the industrial countries, seems to be overly concerned with this question. Whereas the world conferences on the environment, on women, human rights or social issues, which were held in recent years were preceded and accompanied by intensive public debate, food does not seem to be a burning issue. Don't we have mountains of surplus food? people ask. Do we not have to pay our farmers to leave their land idle in order not to add to the glut on the world markets? And hasn't the Green Revolution ended famine even in countries like India which used to be a synonym for hungry people? So where is the problem?

The advance made in agricultural production since beginning against a background of imminent crisis are indeed remarkable. In only 20 years, yields of major crops like rice, maize and wheat in developing countries went up by 80 per cent, outpacing even the rapid increase in population. But this growth in yields has slowed down in recent years, and the aim of "food for all" is once again becoming elusive. About 800 million people still do not have access to enough food to meet their basic daily needs, nearly 200 million children suffer from protein and energy deficiencies, 88 countries—44 of them in Africa—have a deficit in food production.

**Dr. M. Lakshmi Narasaiah**

# Contents

# Chapter 1

# Challenging Traditional Economic Growth

Today, saving the planet is about redefining our economic development models. Stirving towards the fulfilment of basic human rights is an integral part of environmental protection. Without a people-centred development strategy we will fail. Conflicting interests and lack of vision and courage are among the many reasons why it is so hard to meet needs in a world of plenty. We are faced with three major challenges in the 1990s:

- To curb population growth and poverty;
- To search for sustainable production and consumption patterns;
- To promote equity.

Population growth is often associated with poverty. But who causes the major strain on the environment? The 1.2 billion poorest people consume small amounts of the world's resources and contribute little to harmful emissions. They do not cause a heavy burden. The day-to-day struggle for survival of the poorest does, however, undermine their resources, and this causes deaths as population grows beyond the carrying capacity of nature. Here two key elements are essential: to turn from non-renewable to renewable resources, and to minimize use of resources through resource efficiency. We must single out the products and processes that must be phased out and those which may be allowed to expand. Right prices that include the ecological costs will be explored further, together with administrative measures. We are ready to examine the possibilities of using "green tax" reforms to enhance employment and harness pollution and inefficient resources use. By shifting the burden of taxes from labour to environmentally harmful products and processes we might achieve a double benefit.

Transport, waste management, energy and land use are obvious areas that need to be affected by policy changes. Individuals must use their power as green-conscious citizens and shoppers—but, in the end, producers and service providers hold the main key to practical action.

The market must be harnessed to meet people's needs both for present and future generations—starting by making economic policies play by the rules of nature. The World Trade Organisation (WTO) negotiations have provided us with instruments to regulate world trade.

## Getting the Prices Right

Car emissions may be cut drastically, but the rapid increase of new cars nullifies the benefits. Even the most ardent technological optimist must admit that we need new priorities or cuts in some products and services. For example, we must improve public transport and resource-efficient cars—and reduce traffic.

Traditional economic growth models fall short of solving the problem of unemployment. Indeed, 'robots' and wasteful resource use replace people. There are great job-creating possibilities in environment-friendly produces and processes. Striving towards equity within and between nations, and within and between generations, is the major challenge of our time.

The fact that 20 per cent of the world's population consumes 80 per cent of the world's resources has too long been seen as mainly an ethical challenge. Ethics are not easily translated into politics, especially when confronted with economic and market realities. As equity gradually becomes a security issue—as it will, if we do not bridge the gaps within and between nations—it will climb to the top of the political agenda.

Many of the main conflict areas of today are battlefields of resource management. These will expand greatly if we do not turn conference statements of good intention into action. The 30 year old commitment of the rich countries to meet the target of 0.7 per cent of GNP in official Development Assistance remains unmet.

Two hundred years of Western-led development optimism reached its peak in the late 1980s. When the Berlin wall fell, the economic growth models of the rich countries had become the universal recipe. But as more and more people aspire to join the ranks of the middle classes, the resulting environmental stress calls for a halt, or a radical change of course.

The call for new patterns of production and consumption challenges our traditional concepts of economic growth and the focus on materialism in our culture. Neither the industrialised nor the poorer countries are strangers to radical process of change, though the reasons for change are shifting. And we are truly facing challenging and conflict-provoking changes.

No nation by itself can solve the problems we face. Pollution knows no frontiers, but comes to us with the winds and waves. We have become more and more interdependent. If we are to attain sustainable development, we must commit ourselves through international agreements, through an international rule of law, through the development of financial mechanisms and through institutional agreements. We must develop means and tools to enhance collective security and mutual interests.

# Chapter 2

## Can Economic Growth Reduce Poverty?

### *New Findings on Inequality, Economic Growth and Poverty*

Many people still think first of 'economic growth' in relation to poverty reduction. Indeed, their correlation is one of the most-discussed issues of combating poverty. The relationship is of great importance because if there is a clear causal dependency, reducing poverty could fundamentally be limited to measures to promote growth. However, if there was low growth or stagnation it would not be possible to reduce poverty decisively. In the opposite case, that of the phenomena having no causal relation, promising measures to reduce poverty could be taken up even without economic growth.

Hardly anyone now explicitly expresses the view that economic development trickles down automatically to the poor. Practical experience has refuted this assumption dating from the early days of development policy in the 1960s. However, a number of studies show development of growth and a decline in poverty running parallel. On the other hand, there are also examples which show that despite high economic growth, poverty is not reduced markedly. The common answer to the question this raises is thus: Yes, growth can reduce poverty, but only if additional measures oriented on the poor are taken up. This is often termed pro-poor-growth.

But what that means in detail, and whether economic growth as such plays a causal role at all, is not clarified. It is worth taking a look at the arguments on the basis of more recent empirical and theoretical knowledge.

**No Direct Causality Between Growth and Poverty Reduction**

Among the many indicators of poverty, the income of the poor (income poverty) has the closest relationship to economic growth. An increase in gross domestic product and thus national income could, if other factors come into play be linked with an increase in the per capita income of the poor.

Such a relationship between economic growth and the income of the poor, however, cannot be described as causal, as is asserted implicitly time and again by the statement that growth is a necessary but not sufficient precondition for poverty reduction. Insofar as growth and poverty reduction arise at the same time at the end of a process, they exist alongside each other. It would be almost a tautology to say that the former is the cause or part-cause of the latter. Both express the same thing, namely a change in per capita income as well, and both have similar causes. What matters is recognising what these causes are and what specific factors must come into play so that the income of the poor grows too. Growth as a "prerequisite" or "condition" is then no longer the focus; the priority is asking for specific policies that result in higher incomes for the poor. The detour in thinking about growth is not necessary. Since, however, it is based on similar factors, such as fiscal policy/budget structure, employment policy, combating inflation, and institutional development, economic growth can also emerge if poverty is reduced. The difference of views lies in the fact that under the heading 'poverty reduction' the aim is no longer growth, but a purposeful reduction of poverty.

Therefore, in reverse, successful combating of poverty can be seen as being the cause of growth insofar as activating the capabilities of the poor and using their productive capacity of the poor and using their productive capacity triggers economic drive.

**Indirect Causality Between Growth and Poverty Reduction**

So even if economic growth fundamentally has no direct causal impact on poverty, growth still can reduce it indirectly. This is the case when due to positive economic development a government has greater revenue and uses the surplus for combating poverty, for example by providing such public goods as education and health services. Also in these cases, however, growth is not a compelling precondition. Even without growth greater government revenue can be achieved for example by more efficient tax collection. And leeway for social welfare spending can be gained by redistributing the budget, such as by cutting military appropriations. Furthermore, an automatic process is not given because the government can also use surplus funds for non-social purposes.

Creation of jobs due to increased economic activity can be another indirect link between economic growth and income poverty, if such a development generates income and reduces poverty. But also in this case I see no compelling causality because, for instance, industrial jobs are not necessarily open to the really poor. In addition, these positive impacts occur to a considerable extent only in the event of labour-intensive development. In many countries, however, economic growth is achieved by capital-intensive production.

**Inequality, Growth and Income Poverty**

If national incomes, grow, a naïve observer might assume that the income of the poor must also grow along with it. But that would be a statistical fallacy. Even if only the income of the rich grows, this results in macro-economic statistics showing a higher per capita income. What the true conditions are is shown as soon as one divides the population statistically into income groups, such as in fifths, as is usual. It then turns out that the bald figures on average per capita growth can certainly cloak a situation where the income of the richest fifth of the population is growing fast while that of the poorest fifth is stagnating. Despite growth, the gap between the two becomes even wider.

The unequal distribution of income (and of other assets such as property and access to social services), and its connection to poverty reduction and growth has recently returned to the forefront of the debate.

It is obvious that inequality and its changes have direct effects on the poverty situation. Does inequality also have an impact on poverty via its relation to growth, because growth promotes or reduces inequality? Earlier, the predominant view was that rapid growth was linked with at least a temporary increase in inequality, so that a distinct policy of growth initially disadvantaged the poor.

The current dominant view is that growth has no foreseeable effects on inequality and that inequality changes only very slowly, in reverse, however, it is assumed that greater equality is a determinant of growth. According to that view, an indirect relationship between poverty on one side and inequality as a factor dependent upon growth on the other is not given.

That leads to the conclusion that fair distribution has more weight than growth. Fair distribution, however, does not depend upon growth. An appropriate policy is possible at any time, not only after an economic situation has improved. The notion that still shimmers through the debate that "something must be earned first before it can be distributed", is wrong. It is a matter of designing policy and the entire economic process right from the start in such a way that the surplus benefits all including the poor. Important elements of such a policy are, for example, land reform and development of finance systems.

**Relationship of Growth to Poverty**

According to today's conventional wisdom, income poverty expresses only a part of what poverty means. Not least through the voices of the poor themselves, it has become clear that violation of human dignity and rights, a lack of participation in decisions and exclusion from society, unequal treatment of men and women, and vulnerability are also regarded as poverty. For poverty is caused to a great degree by conflicts of power and interests. Income poverty often is not even seen as the greatest problem.

What relationship do these more far reaching characteristics of poverty have to economic growth? A direct relationship of growth to socially-related aspects such as women's inheritance rights, land rights and exclusion from decisions cannot be seen. Considerable improvements in favour of the poor can be achieved here even without economic growth.

Those who see a strong and causal connection between economic growth and poverty reduction must ask themselves what the prospects are for high growth rates and thus for a decline in poverty. Coupling poverty reduction to economic growth is problematic. If only low growth rates are to be expected.

Another question is whether continuous increases in growth are at all desirable and possible in the medium to long term. In this connection, a difference should perhaps be made between developing countries and industrialised nations. But environmental compatibility and availability of resources set limits to growth for both. Some academics assume that industrialised nations have already reached an inherent limit (stagnation theory) and that the high growth rates of earlier years will not return. Moreover, they add, full employment is no longer achievable due to, among other things, an ongoing increase in productivity, and current unemployment cannot be reduced by customary means. In any case, if growth were to be taken as the major benchmark, the prospects for a radical reduction of income poverty around the world would be modest.

## Summing Up

Poverty is a complex problem and reducing it depends upon many interconnected factors that is why poverty cannot be attributed to one main cause nor its reduction based on one main strategy. Economic growth is just one strategic element among many others related to poverty reduction. An indirect causal connection between growth and poverty reduction can only be seen because governments will have a grater scope for action due to economic growth, and if they promote labour-intensive development.

Therefore growth's role in poverty reduction must be put into perspective growth cannot be the first thing that comes to mind, nor is it the golden path to reducing poverty. The simplistic theory of economic growth as the main condition obstructs the bigger picture; it clings to the underlying and ongoing belief in the trickle-down effect. Even if there is no growth or for inherent reasons there can be none, there are promising ways to take on the challenge of mass poverty in the developing countries. Up front, governments and bilateral and multilateral donors must have the political will to design economic, financial and social policies so that they are oriented on poverty in a coherent way—the result can also be economic growth.

# Chapter 3

## Development
### *The People Know Best*

Meetings of the World Bank and the World Trade Organisation has inspired high-mined protest and, on occasion, even vandalism. But this protest and vandalism may miss the point. It is hard to blame those who complain of bullying or blundering by the great institutions of global power. But the poor of the world, especially the poor of developing countries, deserve more than street demonstrations. The poor understand better than anybody the complicated details of their own poverty–the absence of health care, the lack of education, and all the sinister perils to their own safety and well-being. They know the failures of their governments, and of international institutions.

And that is the point: It is the people of the poor countries who will have to apply new knowledge to design and achieve their own development. A country can only develop when its citizens have the freedom to address their own development problems. The obligation of the rich countries, is to give help where they can. And anyone who doesn't see a moral imperative to contribute to a fairer, more prosperous future is free to frame the obligation differently—as self-interest, for example. It will surely serve us better to invest in a peaceful and contented global community than to invite the strife and poverty of unanswered injustice and economic ruin.

Among our relevant conclusions: Powerful institutions of global finance and trade (not least, the World Bank and the World Trade Organisation) can be a source of real promise to poor countries. If governed right, they can help integrate developing economies into the enriching opportunities of global trade and investment. But such promise is often wasted because the very poverty of poor–country governments weakens their ability to negotiate the terms that would serve them best.

Communities in poor countries find themselves at a special disadvantage when it comes to bargaining with foreign investors. Investment can bring growth and spread wealth. It can also threaten human rights and social cohesion, or cultural integrity, and the fragile balance of ecosystems. Nobel economist Amartyasen has spoken powerfully about the intimate relation between development and choice, the subject of his thought-provoking book *Development as Freedom*. Development, Sen argues, "consists of the removal of various types of unfreedoms that leave people with little choice and little opportunity..." He defines freedom as "both the primary end and the principal means of development."

A precondition of this freedom is knowledge—knowledge of the hard facts and the hard science, on which real choices are constructed. Also it is knowledge of good governance—procedures of choice that are effective, responsive and democratic. For budgetary reasons, .rich countries contribution in international development was severely cut in the 1990s. Now, along with others in the rich countries, they have to begin to reinvest in international development.

This means a new commitment to the improvement of lives, and to the future that the north must share with the South. It will be a reinvestment in peace, and in our own prosperity. This remains a matter of obligation, and of sensible self-interest.

# Chapter 4

## Technological Entrepreneurship

### *The New Force for Economic Growth*

**Entrepreneurship has emerged as a major new force for change. The dynamic role of modern small business in economic growth has received fresh recognition worldwide. It is essential to promote entrepreneurship and to mobilize the dynamism of the private sector for accelerated national development. An unbridled private sector may not, however, ensure growth with equity. It is the prime responsibility of governments to create policy frameworks that enable business to apply technology for competitive advantage and for the well-being of the public.**

**The Changing Global Environment**

As agents of change and progress, entrepreneurs start by identifying a market opportunity and matching this with social or technical innovations. They then proceed to mobilize the resources necessary to drive their business concept to its commercial realisation. The development of a product or service with a high-technology content—never easy anywhere, or at today's rapidly-changing global environment. It calls for restructuring the available technology and business development systems and developing the skills needed by a new breed of "techno-entrepreneurs" to transform innovations into market opportunities at home and abroad.

It also requires reorienting the present processes and priorities of technical and economic cooperation among countries.

Amidst the global concerns of environmental preservation, poverty elimination and social development, the practical problems of entrepreneurship are not being properly addressed, even though entrepreneurs will create the bulk of enterprises, jobs and wealth.

A torrent of technology-based goods hits the market every week, ostensibly improving the quality of our lives while simultaneously creating complexity and dislocation. The pace of progress in information technologies, microelectronics, robotics, new materials, biomedical sciences, space science and other advanced technologies quickens, significantly changing the way we live. The growth of markets for these technologies also proceeds apace.

Further, technological change is taking place today against a background of growing intra-national and international disequilibria. While the transformation from State-centred to market-oriented development is opening up enormous opportunities and options, it has also caused severe short-term hardships. In order to survive and prosper in these changing times, India and its enterprises need enlightened government policies, good technical infrastructure and strong cultural roots.

Traditional production factors are giving way to a new paradigm characterised by new patterns of trade, investment and employment, and by informal networking life-long learning and technological entrepreneurship. The manufacturing sector in India continues to be dominated by food products, textiles, chemicals and other traditional industry, mainly in the public sector. However, change is coming, albeit slowly. State enterprises are being corporatised pending privatisation, and the share of knowledge-based and information-related activities in the marketplace is rising perceptibly. Restructuring policies now place emphasis (often purely rhetorical) on the role of the private sector. The legacy of decades of centrally-planned development is generally inimical to private enterprise. In turn, the private sector has been slow to respond to economic liberalisation in India and generally failed to generate the new employment necessary to absorb new entrants to the labour force.

The regulatory problems of an onerous tax structure and administration, poor access to finance and raw materials, over-regulation of labour and land use, pervasive bureaucracy and restricted markets have been significant barriers to entrepreneurial growth.

**Towards Competitive Performance**

The imperative of improved performance has serious implications for India if it is to survive, stay abreast and succeed. It calls for national efforts on systemic efficiency and productivity growth, the move from an investment-driven to an innovation-driven economy and sustained higher-order competitiveness; towards enhanced customer satisfaction at home and penetration of selected markets abroad. Concurrently, governments and business have to address such intractable problems as poverty, corruption and the degradation of the environment.

**Creating New Technology-Based Ventures**

Starting a new business in India is a hazardous task. Problems are compounded when the venture is technology-based:

- Capital requirements are generally larger, while traditional banks are ill-equipped to process the perceived risk. Venture capital generally only becomes an option when the venture has documented the merits of its management, market and innovation.
- Knowledge-based ventures can benefit from linkages to sources of knowledge—e.g. the technical university or research lab. Such mentoring needs to be cultivated.

- Techno-entrepreneurs often have technical skills but usually lack the business management and marketing skills necessary for success. These need to be supplemented.
- In fields where technology is changing rapidly, it is often advantageous to make technology-acquisition arrangements. Sourcing such innovations, negotiating technology licensing agreements and protecting the intellectual property itself require special skills.
- Knowledge-based innovations are inherently more risky than others. The management of this unique risk requires assessment techniques and vision.
- Technology-based ventures often have social and environmental implications, which need to be managed carefully.
- Penetrating a competitive market requires good market intelligence, a good strategic plan and good luck.

**Special Characteristics of "Techno-entrepreneurs"**

The popular misconceptions are that techno-entrepreneurs are born, not made; that they take risks with other people's money and fail more often than they succeeds. In fact, entrepreneur skills can be identified and developed. The entrepreneur is typically an innovator who formulates new solutions to existing problems, mobilizes resources and stimulates others to participate in his or her team. These aptitudes develop over time, often starting in childhood, as the person faces new challenges and learns from failure.

Entrepreneurial opportunities can be found in every industrializing country, community and family. Principal sources of entrepreneurs for knowledge-based ventures are often the university and government research laboratories, the large industrial and military establishments and professional service firms. Some motivations of the entrepreneur are the need to: be independent; create value; contribute to society; earn recognition; become rich or; quite often, simply not to be unemployed. Value-adding ventures with good growth potential can best be developed in an open market and in a culture which supports risk-taking.

The techno-entrepreneur anywhere has the challenge of moving a concept through the prototype and production phases towards creation of a product which meets market needs at a price consistent with the value created and with the ability of customers to pay.

Equally important, the market itself has to be developed and sustained. It is not enough to be first with a better mousetrap if one does not have the skills to educate and reach potential buyers and to set the market standard.

Hence one has to distinguish between innovators and inventors. The inventor is typically a creative person in a quest for knowledge or for producing new products, without determining in advance whether a real market exists for his or her inventions. On the other hand, the innovator draws on existing knowledge and the talents of others to develop or adapt a product or service at a volume and cost that can capture a significant portion of an identified market. The flexibility and creativity of a small entrepreneurial techno-venture may lead to more incremental and break through innovations than can be generated by larger-sized firms in many sectors.

The pace and pattern of India's economic development now depend in large measure on its technical resource base. In this context, the key determinants are the skills to apply technology for enhanced competitiveness, as well as to create tech-based ventures. Techno-entrepreneurs have to be supported by appropriate national structures and international linkages if they are to survive and flourish in an intensely competitive world.

# Chapter 5

# Economics and Sustainable Development

Economists and ecologists were once seen as enemies: environmental protection, it was thought, could only be achieved at the expense of economic growth. The misconception persists at the extremes among both the most fundamentalist Greens and the most ideological free marketers. But increasingly it is now being recognised that development and care for the environment go hand in hand. This interdependence is coalescing in the new and necessary discipline of environmental economics.

Conventional economics patterns have often assumed that growth and technical progress will nullify all resource and environmental limits. Environmental economics recognises that the world's natural capital underpins all development, and that it is rapidly becoming scarcer as human demands exceed the globe's long-term carrying capacity. Government of India has introduced environmental measures over the last two decades, but need to move further towards integrating them into economic policies. There can be no real sustainable development unless environment and development policies are integrated at the very beginning of the decision-making process.

## Quantifying the Environmental Cost

One of the first steps is to work out the true costs of

polluting and depleting the World's natural resources, such as its soil, air and water, the climate and the ozone layer. These have often been regarded as free goods, and it was believed that the world has an infinite capacity to absorb the effects of human activities. Environmental economists, recognising that the social and economic costs of degradation are very great, are trying to quantify them. They say that this will make possible better use of such tools as cost-benefit analysis, environmental impact assessment and risk assessment—and the production of national income accounts which reflect the depletion an degradation of natural resources. As these costs are identified and quantified, economic policy can increasingly be developed with sustainable development as the primary objective. Achieving sustainable development requires industrialized and developing countries to make dramatic changes in national and international policies based on a global partnership. The greenhouse effect, the destruction of the ozone layer, the extinction of species and contamination of the oceans, and other environmental problems, affect us all, no matter which corner of the globe we inhabit.

The first and essential step in overcoming a difficulty is to recognize it and understand it. Concern over the difficulties related to sustainability has led scientists and national and international institutions to study the concept and suggest ways of meeting its many requirements. Indicators have been established to measure pollution levels, soil erosion, salinisation, deforestation and a host of environmental problems. Evaluating the impact of such natural resource-use on ecosystems is a major step towards finding the necessary solutions.

For example, it has become clear, on a macro-economic level, that national accounting systems fail to reflect these effects adequately, Deterioration of the world's rivers, land degradation, air pollution and contamination of the seas are not taken into consideration. Inadequate accounting distorts reality and gives a false idea of the true consequences of growth and production.

On a micro-economic level, much is being done to redefine production costs. Incorporating the cost of waste management and internalizing negative external impacts within production prices are beneficial aspects of the economics of sustainability.

Steps are being taken to evaluate public and commonly held assets and to put a price on them, even though they may not be subject to market forces. These are only in the earliest stage but they will allow for more accurate evaluation of the world's natural capital. Fiscal, market, quota and other instruments are being developed to enforce change in the way in which certain resources are used. Examples include markets for transferable emission quotas or compensatory taxation mechanisms designed to ensure that economic forces act to reduce greenhouse gas emissions. Efforts at impact analysis—and in a general sense, cost-benefit analysis—permit rough estimations of the impact that projects might have on ecosystems.

**Long-term Repercussions**

These instruments carry significant limitations but they are important nevertheless because they attempt to quantify impacts on the natural world and to achieve a more rational use of natural resources. The development of such instruments and evaluation techniques will have significant repercussions in the formulation of sustainable long-term policies. But we must bear in mind that sustainability is not just an economic issue: it is also a political and cultural one.

The concept of sustainability demands as alternative view point in which humankind and the natural world are perceived as a unit—as different yet mutually sustaining aspects of a whole. This perception is not incompatible with progress. It does not renounce development. It simply seeks to affirm life and refuses to discriminate between the means and the end. It understands that happiness cannot be achieved by destructive means. The questions of how to produce and how to consume therefore become extremely important. Neither should be at the expense of the future or of the natural world. Efficiency is not limited to the links between investment, products and prices: it must address the rational use of resources, including environmental and cultural consequences, both in the long- and the short-term.

Very considerable adjustments must be made in the interests of sustainable development. They demand a reassessment of all our activities which cannot, logically, be done overnight. It is a long and continuous process, characterized by steadfastness and compromise.

# Chapter 6

## Population Growth and Jobs

Since mid-century, the world's labour force has more than doubled, from 1.2 billion people to 2.7 billion, outstripping the growth in job creation. As a result, the United Nations International Labour Organisation estimates that nearly 1 billion people, approximately 30 per cent of the global work force, are unemployed or underemployed (working but not earning enough to meet basic needs). Over the next half-century, the world will need to create more than 1.9 billion jobs—all of them in the developing world—just to maintain current levels of employment.

As economists often note, while population growth may boost labour demand (through economic activity and demand for goods), it will most definitely boost labour supply. During the next 50 years, almost 40 million people will enter the global labour force—defined as those between the ages of 15 and 65 seeking work—each year. Between 1995 and 2050, some 1.9 billion additional jobs will need to be created to absorb these new would be workers. The most pressing needs will be found in the world's poorest nations—a sobering example of the vicious cycle linking poverty and population growth.

As the children of today represent the workers of tomorrow, the interaction between population growth and jobs is most acute in nations with young populations. Nations such as Peru, Mexico, Indonesia, and Zambia with more than half their population below the age of 25 will feel the burden of this labour flood. In the Middle East and Africa, 40 per cent of the population is under the age of 15. Since new entrants into the labour force were born at least 15 years ago, measures to reduce population growth have a delayed effect on the growth of the labour force, highlighting the urgency of taking action on population.

Nowhere is the employment challenge greater than in Africa, where at least 40 per cent of the population lives in absolute poverty. Although 8 million people entered the sub-Saharan workforce in 1997, by 2030 this resource-scarce region will have to absorb more than 17 million new entrants each year. Over the next half-century, Nigeria's labour force is projected to grow by 246 per cent and Ethiopia's will soar by 337 per cent—both faster than growth of the general population. At current growth rates, the size of the labour force in sub-Saharan Africa will more than triple by 2050.

As a result of unprecedented population growth and increasing acceptance of female participation in the workforce, the number of people seeking jobs in the Middle East and North Africa, a region already plagued by double-digit unemployment rates, will double in the next 50 years. In Algeria, where unemployment stands at 22 per cent, the labour force is growing at a staggering 4.2 per cent annually, and the number seeking work will more than double by 2050. Egypt alone will need to create 26 million more jobs by 2050 as its total population hits 115 million.

Nations throughout Asia will also see phenomenal increases in the numbers seeking work, including Pakistan, where the workforce will grow from 70 million in 1998 to 205 million by 2050. Over the next 25 years, India will add nearly 10 million to its workforce each year. During the same period, China will add nearly 6 million annually due to population growth alone, compounding the work shortages caused by the current flood of migrants to China's coastal cities and by massive layoffs—estimated at more than 30 million—as state-run operations are scaled back.

Nations are hard-pressed to educate and train rapidly growing numbers of young people in marketable skills for the global workplace. Moreover, meeting the basic needs of a growing population draws scarce foreign exchange and other resources from investments in education and job creation. Throughout the world, young people entering the workforce are increasingly faced with unemployment and social marginalisation. In most societies, unemployment rates for those under 25 are substantially higher than for older people.

Surplus farmland once served as a traditional source of employment for growing populations, as new land could be ploughed to generate work and income. However, global percapita Greenland has dropped by half and considerably more in certain nations since 1950. Moreover, the mechanisation of agriculture fuels the exodus of job seekers into the world's urban areas, where unemployment is often most acute, heavily reliant on natural capital in the past, future job creation will require massive amounts of financial capital to jump-start the industrial and service sectors.

As the balance between the demand and supply of labour is tipped by population growth, wages—the price of labour—tend to decrease. And in a situation of labour surplus, the quality of jobs may not improve as fast for workers will settle for longer hours, fewer benefits and less control over work activities.

Employment is the key to obtaining food, housing, health services, and education, in addition to providing self-respect and self-fulfilment. Rising numbers of unemployed people could drive global poverty and hunger to precarious levels, fueling political instability.

# Chapter 7

## Food for the Billions

Will there be enough food to feed 8 billion people who will live on earth in 25 years' time? Surprisingly few people, at least in the industrial countries, seems to be overly concerned with this question. Whereas the world conferences on the environment, on women, human rights or social issues, which were held in recent years were preceded and accompanied by intensive public debate, food does not seem to be a burning issue. Don't we have mountains of surplus food, people ask. Do we not have to pay our farmers to leave their land idle in order not to add to the glut on the world markets? And hasn't the Green Revolution ended famine even in countries like India which used to be a synonym for hungry people? So where is the problem?

The advance made in agricultural production since beginning against a background of imminent crisis are indeed remarkable. In only 20 years, yields of major crops like rice, maize and wheat in developing countries went up by 80 per cent, outpacing even the rapid increase in population. But this growth in yields has slowed down in recent years, and the aim of "food for all" is once again becoming elusive. About 800 million people still do not have access to enough food to meet their basic daily needs, nearly 200 million children suffer from protein and energy deficiencies, 88 countries—44 of them in Africa—have a deficit in food production.

Everyone wants to increase food security. The definition is that "food be available at all times, that all persons have means of access to it, that it be nutritionally adequate in terms of quantity, quality and variety, and that it be acceptable within the given culture". To achieve this goal, more food must be produced—much more, because we must not only adequately feed the 5.8 billion people already on earth, but also the additional two billion who will be added to world population in the next 25 years. Critics argue that the problem is not one of production alone, but one of poverty elimination. People are not hungry because there is no food, but because they have no money to buy it, these critics say. Available resources must be better distributed to end hunger in the world.

However, even if we succeed to eliminate poverty in the next few decades—a feat which appears highly unlikely—there would still be the need to boost production, because with rising incomes people also want to eat more and better food including meat. As can already be observed in the countries of East Asia, the newly acquired wealth leads to higher consumption levels which puts additional strains on available resources are getting scarcer. Agricultural lands are being degraded at alarming speed by erosion, salinity, desertification or disappear altogether due to urban or infrastructure development. It has been estimated that 40 per cent of productive land now has diminished capacity to supply benefits to humanity due to direct human impacts of land use. Water for agricultural purposes is getting scarcer almost everywhere, and there are hardly any land reserves to be brought into production to widen the agricultural base.

In this situation, there is no alternative to increasing and improving production from the existing land area. This can only be done through research which finds the best varieties which will bring the highest yields at the lowest cost to the environment. Sustainable agriculture is the key notion—one that maintains bio-diversity, uses as little chemical inputs as possible and does not over-exploit water and soil resources.

In recent years, agricultural research has been neglected, partly because of the erroneous belief that with mountains of meat and lakes of milk further production increases were not desirable. Since global grain production has stagnated and world stocks have reached an alarmingly low level last year, there has been a noticeable change of mind. To raise the awareness among governments around the world that promotion of agriculture is urgent if hunger is to be avoided in the next century.

Important work is already being done by the international agricultural research institutes which promoted the Green Revolution in the sixties and seventies and are now again in the forefront of finding solutions to the daunting task of feeding 8 billion people by the year 2020. The International Rice Research Institute (IRRI) in the Philippines, the Maize and Wheat Research Institute (CIMMYT) in Mexico or institutes like ICARDA in Syria and ICRISAT in India which work on agriculture in semi-arid and dry areas, are all seeking solutions to the problem of raising production while at the same time preserving the environment. These institutions as well as national agricultural research institutions need all the support from the public and, of course, appropriate funding, to help them accomplish their task.

The scientists are optimistic that they can develop the varieties and farming systems which will allow mankind to feed everyone on earth well into the next century. But the task is not for the scientists alone. An economic and political order must also be in place which makes it possible to eradicate poverty and allow everyone to enjoy the benefits that science can offer. Feeding the billions is, therefore not only a scientific, but first and foremost a political task.

# Chapter 8

## Food Production

During the last 25 years, world agriculture successfully expanded food production faster than population growth. This can continue for the next 25 years and beyond, if appropriate action is taken. Although world food stocks are currently low and grain prices high, the world is not about to run out of food. We can produce enough food for future generation if we choose to do so.

The widespread food insecurity, unhealthy living conditions, and abject and absolute poverty in many developing countries are already threatening global stability. Failure to assure sustainable food security will foster the very conditions that will further destabilise and polarise the world in the years to come with tremendous consequences for all people.

### The Basic Facts

Poverty is widespread in developing countries, with over 1.1 billion people living on a dollar a day or less per person. Human resource development in developing countries is lagging: 1 billion people lack access to health services, 1.3 billion do not have access to adequate sanitation systems, and one-third of primary school enrolls drop out by Grade 4. Natural resources, upon which future food production depends, are being degraded at alarming rates: almost 2 billion hectares of land have been degraded in the past 50 years: about 180 million hectares of forests have been converted to other uses during the 1980s, marine fisheries are collapsing around the world, and regional and seasonal water shortage afflict many developing countries. Improved appropriate technology is essential to increase productivity. Yet low-income food deficit developing countries are grossly under investing in agricultural research and many are reducing their support.

It calls for sustained action in six priority areas. First, we must selectively strengthen the capacity of developing country governments to perform appropriate functions such as establishing or clarifying property rights, promoting private-sector competition in agricultural markets, and maintaining appropriate macro-economic environments. Predictability, transparency and continuity in policy-making and enforcement must be pursued.

**Investing in People**

Second, we must invest more in poor people in order to enhance their productivity, health, and nutrition. It is not only unethical but economically wasteful that a large share of the world's population is malnourished, illiterate, sick, and without access to productive resources. Access to primary education, primary health care, reproductive care and family planning information, and clean water and sanitation must be assured for all people. Access by the poor to productive resources and remunerative employment must be improved. Empowerment of women must be supported.

Third, we must accelerate agricultural productivity. Agriculture is the life blood of the economy in low-income developing countries. In those countries, it provides upto three-quarters of all employment and half of all incomes. There are very strong links between agricultural productivity increases and broad-based economic growth in the rest of the economy. Agriculture is an engine of growth in low-income developing countries. National and international agricultural research systems must be mobilised to develop improved technologies focussed on developing countries, and extension systems must be strengthened to disseminate the improved technologies and techniques. Low-income countries currently spend less than 0.5 per cent of the value of agricultural production on agricultural research compared to 2 per cent spent on agricultural research in middle and high-income countries. An increase of agricultural research expenditures in low-income countries to at least 1 per cent of the value of a agricultural output is urgently needed, with a longer term target of 2 per cent. National agricultural research must be supported by a vibrant international agricultural research system that undertakes research with large international benefits applicable across boundaries. Current investments in international agricultural research are grossly inadequate to provide the support needed by developing countries. It is of critical importance that agricultural research result in reduced unit costs of production. Such cost reductions will make food economically accessible to low-income consumers, and permit producer incomes to increase. To assure relevance of research and appropriate distribution of responsibilities, interactions between public sector agricultural research systems, farmers, private enterprises, and NGOs must be strengthened.

Fourth, we must assure sustainability in agricultural production and sound management of natural resources. Farmers, local communities, and governments must be encouraged to establish and enforce systems of rights to use and manage natural resources, to improve the way water is allocated and used, to reverse land degradation where it has occurred, to reduce the use of chemical pesticides and promote integrated pest management programmes, and to implement integrated soil fertility programmes in areas with low soil fertility. Local control over natural resources must be strengthened and local capacity for organisation and management improved. Investments in less-favoured geographical areas, that is, areas with agricultural potential, irregular rainfall patterns, and fragile soils must be expanded. Most poor people in developing countries reside in rural areas, and most rural poor reside in less-favoured areas. Yet, most investments, including agricultural research investments, still focus on the more-favoured areas. If we are serious about reducing poverty and protecting the natural resource base, the balance between the less-favoured and more-favoured areas must be redressed.

Fifth, we must reduce food-marketing costs in low-income developing countries. The cost of bringing food from the producer to the consumer is very high in many of these countries. Efficient, effective, and low-cost agricultural markets must be developed in order to bring these costs down. Inefficient state-run firms in agricultural input markets must be phased out; investment in developing and maintaining infrastructure, especially in rural areas, must be forthcoming; policies and institutions that favour large-scale, capital-intensive market agents over small-scale, labour-intensive ones must be removed; development of small-scale credit and savings institutions must be facilitated, and technical assistance to create or strengthen small-scale, labour-intensive competitive rural enterprises must be provided.

Sixth, we must expand and realign international development assistance. Many years ago, industrialised countries had agreed to allocate at least 0.7 per cent of the gross national product (GNP) to international assistance. Most countries have not reached or do not maintain this target. No only must the industrialised countries increase international development assistance to reach the 0.7 per cent target, but they must realign it to low-income developing countries. Also contrary to the middle and higher-income developing countries, the poorest countries are not able to gain access to capital from the rapidly expanding international commercial capital market. Developing countries in turn must seek measures to diversify sources of external funding, stem capital flight; and improve the effectiveness of the aid they receive.

# Chapter 9

## Food First

By the time this day is over, about 40,000 human beings—mostly children—will have died from hunger, malnutrition and related causes. Today and everyday the deaths will mount, reaching an annual toll of 13 to 18 million. Few of these people will have been caught up in famine or other emergencies. Most will have suffered from a "silent" assault—the kind that seldom makes the headlines, but which claims its victims just as relentlessly.

It is intolerable that such deprivation and suffering should be allowed to exist in a world of potential food plenty. Having enough food is fundamental to all else. At the most basic level, this may entail humanitarian relief to assist people in emergency situations. In the transition from relief to development, however, we must look at systems for ensuring that societies have the capacity to produce or purchase the food they need and that it is accessible to all.

Sustainable food security fuses the goals of household food security and sustainable agriculture; it requires both. It requires looking not only at the aggregate supply of food, but also at the distribution of income and land, and at other issues: Do people have enough income to buy food? Enough land to grow their own food? Does the food distribution system deliver food where it is needed? How much food is wasted due to inadequate distribution systems? What are the implications of trends in population growth for future food needs? What is the status of women in society, and what opportunities do women have to alter rapid population growth rates? What is being done to regenerate the resource base for food production? These questions need to be asked and answered in every country.

The challenge of sustainable food security is immense, and it is growing. One billion people—20 per cent of the global population—are too poor to obtain enough food to sustain normal work. Half a billion are too poor to obtain the food needed for healthy growth of children and minimal activity of adults. Today's failure to feed people, however, may be but a prologue to a much larger failure in the future. Given likely population increases, world food output must triple over the next 50 years if the world's people are to have a nutritionally adequate diet. It will be difficult enough to achieve this expansion under favourable circumstances, and conditions may be far from favourable.

For example, according to recent estimates an area of about 1.2 billion hectares—the size of China and India combined—has experienced moderate to extreme soil deterioration since World War II as a result of human activities. Over three-fourths of that deterioration has occurred in the developing regions from causes such as overgrazing, deforestation, land clearing, unsound agricultural practices and increased soil salinity and water logging, largely from irrigation. Other environmental threats to the agricultural resource base include loss of water and genetic resources, adverse effects of pesticides and climate change, both local and global.

At the most aggregate level, the required increase in food production could be met if production grew at the historic average, that is, at the two per cent per annum rate achieved over the past half-century. But is this realistic? To produce three times more calories, all the land currently under cultivation around the world would, within 50 years, have to attain levels of productivity as high as those exhibited by the very best cropland today.

To this challenge add the possibility of diminished returns from the technological, energy and other inputs that have made agriculture so successful. Some experts believe that most of the potential for increased output of cereals—from improved plant varieties, from increased use of pesticides and fertilizers and from expanding the area under irrigation—has already been captured.

Viewed from this perspective, the goal of achieving sustainable food security in the decades ahead emerges as one of the greatest challenges humanity has ever faced. Agricultural output must be tripled, and people must have the income to buy the food they need. The erosion of the resource base must be halted and then reversed. Failure on any of these fronts will yield unprecedented human suffering.

What will it take to achieve sustainable food security? Obviously, the effort will have to be immense, both in size and complexity. Outlined below are a few simple (but no easy) steps that are absolutely essential elements of serious effort.

First, as citizens of the world, we must all come to see sustainable food security as a fundamental aspect of global peace and human security. This goes well beyond merely denouncing the use of food as a weapon.

Second, we must adopt concrete international goals, such as reducing world hunger by half over the next 10 years. We will never achieve the goal of sustainable food security unless we aim at specific milestones, and assess rigorously our progress in moving toward them.

Third, we must forge a true global partnership, a compact for sustainable food security. All countries—rich and poor—have important roles and responsibilities. There must be reciprocal responsibilities among nations, not one-way transfers.

Fourth, we must see deterioration of the agricultural resource base—terrestrial, aquatic and climatic—for what it is: a major threat to development and a major source of economic loss. Farmers are the largest group of environmental decision-makers in the world. We must ensure that they have the means to make sustainable development a reality where it counts—in the fields and fisheries.

Fifth, we must empower the people who work the land and who keep it productive. They are in the best position to decide the most appropriate ways to graft new technology onto their own traditional knowledge of seed selection, plant protection and nutrient-cycling. Special emphasis should be given to the role of women, the main providers for two-thirds of the poorest households in the developing world, as well as the producers of 60 per cent of all food grown and consumed locally.

Sixth, we must build the capacities of developing countries, both in government and in civil society. Capacity-building means empowerment for self-reliance. It means strengthening national capacities, both inside and outside government. This is essential for recognition and analysis of problems, for decision-making on courses of action and for management of systems and processes.

Seventh, not only must we build capacity in developing countries, we must also create linkages among researchers in industrial and developing countries. This will help minimize the time lag between discovery and practical utilisation. In addition, analysts from various countries must work together to examine future food security issues with different scenarios of population growth, agricultural productivity, markets and trade, climate change, loss of soil and bio-diversity and, last but not least, political instability, in order to devise options for rational choices.

We know a good deal about how to rid the world of the scourge of hunger, and how to begin to move toward sustainable food security on a global basis. We know that economic growth and prosperity are necessary, though not sufficient, conditions for eradicating hunger. We also know that developing efforts must encompass not only food production, but also socio-economic factors, including sustainable livelihoods for poor families, the implications of population growth rates, the status of women and girls and so forth. We also know that good words are not enough. Now more than ever before it is crucial that we marshal the political will to achieve our goals.

# Chapter 10

# India's Food Challenge

Is India's population growing disproportionately to its food supply? Will famine once again hit millions of people? Most agriculture experts agree that a Malthusian crisis is not likely to occur in the near term. The reason; the overall food situation in India has been characterized by a large increase in regional output since the famine-ravaged 1960s.

At that time, the food situation was described as "desperate" in India. Famine had plagued India's Bihar state in the sixties. International food specialists predicted further famine because food production looked as if it would lag far behind population growth. Instead, average crop yields per acre soared, thanks to the introduction of high-yielding varieties of rice and wheat and to expanded irrigation and chemical fertilizer use. It has been called the "Green Revolution".

**Double Role of Irrigation**

The keys to the higher food production have been irrigation, the adoption of high-yielding varieties (HYVs) of foodgrains and the increased use of modern inputs such as fertilizers. Irrigation has played a double role, it has not only helped raise yields through synergistic interaction with HYVs and fertilizers, but has also contributed to considerable increases in harvested area by enabling higher cropping intensity.

Still, there are ominous clouds on Indian food horizon. In light of the region's high population growth, increased urban sprawl and rampant environmental degradation, there are signs that hunger problems could loom unless action is taken by Indian's and international development agencies.

**Shrinking Base**

The favourable food supply situation is likely to disappear within the next decade, due to a shrinking resource base. The earlier decades had witnessed a natural resources-based growth strategy as there was adequate land and water resources for development. But this is fast disappearing due to urbanisation, industrialisation and ecological degradation. We should also remember that about 50 per cent of food production is from rainfed lands and a few years of drought could alter the food security which we now enjoy. The high costs of irrigation and land development, coupled with low commodity prices, are also hampering required investments and these effects will be seen in the next decade.

"By the year 2030, India will have to produce 60 per cent more rice with much fewer resources. Clearly, there will be a major challenge for scientists and policy-makers to meet the increased food demand. India's population is growing 2 per cent a year, making the challenges for regional food security a daunting task.

The solution for meeting future food demand will be breakthroughs in science and technology since yield levels have reached a plateau and are even showing signs of decline. The possibilities through biotechnology and genetic engineering are exciting and can herald another "green revolution". This is the only hope for avoiding the Malthusian dilemma.

In gauging the region's population-food squeeze, it is useful to look first at its swelling population. India—the world's second populous region contains several states with high population growth rates.

**Ironic Problem**

Rapid population growth dilutes and impedes economic development. An increase in the population base puts greater pressure on finite resources, both financial and natural, and, in the context, worsening of income distribution, increased poverty incidence and environmental degradation.

Moreover, there is the ironic problem, that although rapid population growth increases poverty, poverty encourages larger families through its impact on access to education and decreased prospects for child survival.

If population growth is uncontrolled, the economic and social consequences are:

- ecological imbalance, with greater pressure on natural resources;
- increased urban crowding, with increases in demand for municipal services and infrastructure;
- a more unequal income distribution, particularly as labour supply outpaces job creation;
- signs of mass poverty, including high infant and child mortality rates, high levels of child malnutrition and hunger, poor school performance, unemployment and underemployment.

**Bleak Prospects**

Existing population growth rate is unsustainable, even for the relatively near future. Unless population growth rate is kept within manageable limits, the prospects for creating acceptable standards of living for low-income groups in India will be bleak.

The Indian population is growing more rapidly than ever before and will continue to do so for at least four decades. Indeed, without major technological breakthroughs and changes in patterns of consumption, even the most optimistic population growth projections are likely to be accompanied by increase in poverty, hunger and environmental degradation.

Whether we look at population, the environment or development, the next 10 years will be critical for our future. The decisions we make or don't take will widen or narrow our options for a century to come. They could decide the fate of the earth as a home for human beings.

# Chapter 11

## Less Food Security in the South

Combating hunger and poverty is the central point of Bread for the world' s mandate. In our view, that is not so much about the quantity of food produced in the world. On the one hand, it's about its fair distribution and, on the other, the access of poor people to chances of jobs. Put another way, it's to do with access to purchasing power. In the case of agriculture, that is bound up with the question of how food is produced. Whether the technologies applied maximize employment or replace work with capital.

### Hunger though Surplus

The question of production, employment and distribution are tied closely to the general conditions for development. It is certainly not exclusively external economic conditions, which account for hunger and under-development. Structural deficits, political conditions and wrong policies in Third World countries have become increasingly clear. However, it can still be noted that global economic framework conditions remain enormously important for the development of agriculture in the Third World.

Twenty years ago, Bread for the world publicly expounded the thesis "Hunger through surplus" and had to take much criticism for it—above all from agro-economists. But since then the contradiction between the ever-growing mountains of agricultural surpluses in the northern hemisphere and the increasing dependence on food imports of the South has become ever more apparent. Out of 120 poor developing countries, 107 today are net importers of food.

The North's surpluses of dairy products, grain, beef and sugar—which because of their production costs are exorbitantly expensive—thrust their way on to world market and destroy local supply systems (which are cheap because of subsidies), regional trade flows, and the sales possibilities of potential Third World agro-exporters. Thus, the surpluses contribute to the situation that in many developing countries a policy of neglecting local agriculture can be continued with impurity.

Initially, the promise to work on the yawning gap between hunger and surplus in the world was upfront on WTO agenda. But the pattern of explanation was well simplified. It said that surpluses arose only in those countries, which supported their agriculture positively and, in fact, partly excessively. And that agricultural deficiencies in countries of the South were caused mainly by deprivation of resources and capital. However, the concept of not only reducing neglect of agriculture in the South but also its oversubsidising in the North to a sensible degree and thereby eliminating their distortions of world markets had a great intellectual attraction. At any rate, it promised more justice in agriculture.

### Subsidies Can Make Sense

To avoid misunderstandings, we have nothing against the support of agriculture in Europe. Above all not when it is done for social, ecological or agriculturally beneficial reasons.

On the contrary, agriculture's important role for food security, the sustainable handling of natural resources, the settlement of rural areas, and the social function of family farms justify a special position for it is economic life, including protection and support.

But that must not be carried so far that surpluses are produced with the help of dubious production methods and then dumped on the world market at markedly less than cost price, causing incalculable damage in the poor countries. On the other hand, purposeful promotion of rural development is a prerequisite and model for greater self-sufficiency worldwide, especially in Third World countries.

**Complementary Functions of World Markets**

The poor countries of the South have no alternative than to become self-sufficient in food. The World markets can at best assume complementary functions. The countries would take indeterminable risks if they integrated themselves completely in the world markets, and thereby wanted to make themselves dependent upon global agro-markets. These are and will remain extremely unreliable factors that are conditioned by enormous fluctuations in prices and quantities, the powerful, and in many cases obscure, influences of multinational concerns, the manifold political interventions in the agricultural scene in most countries, and the dangers of social and ecological dumping.

But when we now look at the results of the WTO, we are disappointed. The development question and the balancing of hunger and surplus are finally no longer on the agenda. Programmes to increase food production in the poor countries were not the priority of the negotiations. The liberalisation of agro-policies in the developing countries would have meant making the disadvantaging of their farmers the subject of international negotiations. That did not happen.

On the contrary, the concepts developed with an eye on the reform of agricultural policy in the North, which target the reduction of the support level, are to be transferred to the South without questions. To be sure, there are a whole number of exemptions for the poorest developing countries. But the WTO results have also set the trend there, namely the dismantlement of subsides. We cannot understand how such a thing can be demanded as a policy programme, especially for Africa. Support for African agriculture is largely absent, i.e. there is absolutely nothing to dismantle. That's why many international conferences repeatedly emphasise the need for the countries to achieve a greater degree of self-sufficiency in food by stronger support of their agriculture.

**Agro-Dumping**

Certainly, some changes have been made in the North's agro policy system, which will also have positive impacts on world agricultural markets. However, also here we must express our disappointment. Agricultural dumping will continue. The only difference will be the new policy instrument of direct transfer of income instead of subsidised grain prices. The opening of markets in future will hardly go beyond the current preference conditions.

The entire set of WTO agreements, however, bears the imprint of the two agricultural superpowers, the USA and the European Union, which make mutual concessions and coordinate their agricultural policies. But one hears nothing about the target of freeing the world agricultural market from unnecessary distortions and ensuring justice. The intention of the agro-superpowers was solely to defend their global market shares.

The development aid agencies cannot close their eyes to these problems. On the contrary, in future they must make very much greater effort in suggesting better goals, programmes and instruments which are capable of forming a policy that can then be included in the agenda of the next rounds of negotiations. We may perhaps have slept a bit through the past WTO talks. Therefore it is even more important that we get very much more involved from now on.

# Chapter 12

## Food Security

### *Availability and Access to Food*

The world food situation has never been better. Enough food is being produced today that, if it were evenly distributed, no one should have to go hungry. World food production is increasing faster than population growth: per capita production increased by 5 per cent during the 1980s. Real food prices are at historic lows and have been declining for some time now. Yields of major cereals have more than doubled in the past three decades. These trends have contributed to complacency in some quarters regarding the world food situation.

Yet, more than 700 million people in the developing world do not have access to sufficient food to lead healthy and productive lives. More than 180 million children are underweight. Diseases of hunger and malnutrition are widespread. The desire to satisfy food needs has, in combination with increasing population densities and inadequate agricultural intensification, led to much degradation of environmentally fragile lands, such as forests and steep hillsides.

Over the next 20-30 years, farmers and policy-makers in developing countries will be challenged to provide food at affordable prices for almost 100 million more people every year—the largest annual population increase in history. Moreover, they will have to increase food production from more productive use of the land and without further degradation of natural resources: area expansion is no longer a feasible option in most of the world.

What future food security will look like depends not on exogenous factors over which we have no control but on the decisions and actions taken by the major players: households, private- and public-sector agencies, governments, and the international community. If we continue to act as we have in the 1980s and early 1990s, more people will suffer from food insecurity it will be because some or all of these players failed to act in an appropriate and timely manner.

**Feeding the World: Availability and Access to Food**

There is enough food in the world today to feed everyone, if it were evenly distributed. Availability of daily food energy per capita in the developing countries as a whole increased by 0.7 per cent per year during the 1980s.

Twenty-five developing countries, including about half of the African countries, were unable to assure sufficient food energy (2,200 calories per person per day) for their populations at the end of the 1980s even if available food energy were evenly distributed within each country. This is down from 45 countries at the end of the 1970s.

However, available food is neither evenly distributed nor fully consumed. Availability of enough food at global, regional, or national levels does not necessarily mean that everyone is well fed. For people to be food secure—that is, to have access at all times to the food required for a healthy and productive life—there must be both availability of food and access to food. Access to food by households (and individuals) is conditioned by poverty: the poor usually lack adequate means to secure access to food.

Over 1.1 billion people in developing countries were living in poverty in 1993, more than 500 million in conditions of extreme poverty. South Asia is the home of about 50 per cent of the developing world's poor—more than 500 million people. Another 15 per cent are found in East Asia, 19 per cent in Sub-Saharan Africa, and 10 per cent in Latin America and the Caribbean. The prevalence of poverty (the proportion of each region's population that is poor) is very high—about 50 per cent—in South Asia as well as in Sub-Saharan Africa.

Today, there are more than 700 million people who do not have access to sufficient food to meet their needs for a healthy and productive life; they often go hungry, adults and children also suffer from diseases associated with hunger and poverty. For almost one-fifth of the total population of developing countries to be chronically hungry tarnishes the images of a world that is now considered food-secure because it produces enough food.

Great progress has been made in meeting food needs during the last 30 years. For instance, the number of underfed people declined from an estimated 976 million in 1974-76 to 786 million in late 1980s. But the problem is far from solved. Keeping up with increasing needs and demands due to population growth, income increases, and dietary changes is itself a formidable challenge.

Hunger and food insecurity have a significant effect on health and nutrition of both adults and children. They can lead to growth failure in children. About 184 million preschool children in developing countries were underweight in 1994. About 55 per cent of these underweight children were found in South Asia and another 16 per cent in Sub-Saharan Africa. The proportion of children that are underweight is higher in South Asia (almost 60 per cent), but it is also significant in Sub-Saharan Africa (30 per cent) and Southeast Asia (31 per cent). It is worrisome that the number of underweight children in Sub-Saharan Africa during the 1980s from 20 million to 28 million is particularly striking.

In addition to energy deficiencies, micro nutrient deficiencies are also widespread in the developing world.

About 14 million pre-school children (under the age of five years) have eye damage as a result of Vitamin-A deficiency. Ten million of these children are found in Southeast Asia. Between 250,000 and 500,000 pre-school children go blind each year due to Vitamin-A deficiency, two-thirds of these children die within months of going blind. Many more children are mildly affected. Recently research has shown that even mild deficiencies can increase mortality significantly. Vitamin-A deficiencies are closely linked to diet, which can be influenced by agricultural research and policy.

Iron deficiency affects about 1 billion people in the world, particularly children and women of reproductive age. Iron deficiency leads to anaemia, which, if not checked, can diminish learning capacity and increase morbidity and mortality. In the developing countries, about 370 million women between 15 and 49 years of age—42 per cent of this population group—where anaemic in the 1980s. Almost one-half were in South Asia. And there are tentative indications from South Asia and Sub-Saharan Africa that the prevalence of anaemia is rising in non-pregnant adult women of reproductive ages.

In Sub-Saharan Africa, this trend is undoubtedly associated with deterioration in general standards of living, including increased poverty and food insecurity. Anaemia partly arises from diets insufficient in iron, which again could be addressed through agricultural research and policy. For example, a possible reason why iron deficiency and anaemia are going up in South Asia may lie in the decrease in production of iron rich pulses during that same period, which in part reflects the larger research input into competing crops such as wheat in South Asia. This emphasizes the importance of considering the effects on diet and thus on health and nutrition in setting research priorities for yield-increasing research.

South Asia is the home of about half of the developing world's hungry and food-insecure people, but this population group is growing rapidly in Sub-Saharan Africa. Much of the poverty and food insecurity is in rural areas, mainly in low-potential areas such as arid zones, but urban poverty is also growing rapidly.

**Four Key Factors will Influence Future Food Production and Consumption**

Global and regional food production and consumption during the next 10-20 years will be influenced by a large number of factors. Changes in the following four sets of factors are likely to particularly important:

1. Economic growth and economic policies;
2. Population growth and urbanisation;
3. Rural infrastructure, agricultural production technology, and access to modern inputs; and
4. Natural resource management and environmental consideration.

The expected impact of each of these factors on future food production and consumption is considerable.

**Economic Growth and Economic Policies**

Economic growth must resume in the developing world, especially in Sub-Saharan Africa. To support such growth, it is critical to:

- complete structural adjustment and economic reforms;
- remove external barriers to growth such as trade distortions and subsidies in developed countries;
- liberalise trade and remove market distortions;
- enhance access by the poor to land capital, and technology;
- expand investment in rural infrastructure, health, education, and agricultural research and technology;
- facilitate sustainability in agricultural production; and

- reverse the decline in international assistance to agriculture.

Growth in real per capita income during the 1980s was disappointing for developing countries as a whole. However, the low average rate of growth covers large variations among regions. The high rates of economic growth in Asia are expected to continue through the 1990s, while incomes in Sub-Saharan Africa are expected to keep pace with population growth.

Future economic growth depends on internal policies as well as on the international policies as well as on the international environment. The extent to which current structural adjustment and economic reforms in Latin America, Sub-Saharan Africa, the Commonwealth of Independent States (CIS), Eastern Europe, and selected countries in Asia and the Middle East are carried to successful completion at an appropriate speed and sequence is of paramount importance for future economic growth in those countries.

Closely related to this issue is the question of the most appropriate role of the state in a market-oriented economy with inappropriate institutions, poor infrastructure, and insufficient experience by the private sector in dealing effectively in a competitive market environment. Over-reaction to past failures such as excessive and inappropriate state intervention may cause governments to take on a passive role where intervention is needed to assure that the markets function effectively and to deal with outside influences on the economy.

Future economic growth will also depend on the international trade environment, including trade distortions by developed countries, and access to external aid. Import restrictions for agricultural and non-agricultural products in Japan, the European Union, and the United States, along with domestic agricultural subsidies and implicit and explicit export subsidies for agricultural products, are of particular concern.

**Population Growth and Urbanisation**

If progress in economic growth is not to be undermined by rapid population growth and excessive urbanisation, effective population and migration policies are necessary to complement growth-oriented policies. Such policies must focus on:

- universal access to family planning information and technology; and
- incentives to reduce rural-urban migration, such as provision of employment in rural areas and stimulation of agricultural and non-agricultural growth in rural areas.

Although the annual growth rate is falling for the world as a whole, the population increase during the next 20-30 years, of slightly less than 100 million people a year, will be the largest ever. Approximately 97 per cent of this increase is projected to occur in the Third World, with Africa alone accounting for 34 per cent of the growth. Thus although reductions in annual population growth rates have begun to occur in Asia and Latin America, they are insufficient to counter the absolute increases. Population growth rates of these magnitudes will greatly increase the need for food and other basic necessities.

**Rural Infrastructure, Agricultural Production Technology, and Access to Modern Inputs**

Continued progress in all three of these areas is critical to future food security.

- Resources must be committed to infrastructure construction and maintenance. Labour-intensive public works programmes are a viable mechanism for building roads, reforesting areas, and engaging in soil conservation projects, while creating employment and income in rural areas.
- International and national agricultural research must continue to develop yield-enhancing production

technology, especially in maize, millet, and other crops, as well as build tolerance or resistance in crops to pests and adverse climatic conditions.

- Farmer access to modern inputs must be facilitated through provision of credit and technical assistance. Inputs must be made available to all farmers on time and in required amounts.

The importance of investments in rural infrastructure within the context of rapid urbanisation has already been established. Even without rapid urban growth, however, such investments are needed in many developing countries, particularly the poorest ones, to facilitate agricultural and rural development. Improved rural infrastructure enhances access to export markets, modern production inputs, and consumer goods. It reduces marketing costs, promotes exchange between intracountry markets, reduces spatial and temporal price distortions, and, in general, increases efficiency in production and marketing.

However, while essential, effective rural infrastructure alone is not enough to assure agricultural and rural development and rapid increases in food production in developing countries. Yield enhancing production technology is of critical importance. Although opportunities for expansion of agricultural production into lands not currently under cultivation still exist in some countries, such opportunities are so limited that they would probably not be able to counter losses of current agricultural lands to alternative uses on a global level. Furthermore, attempts to expand agricultural production into new lands would, in most cases, require large investments in technology, tools and materials and would increase the risk of land degradation and deforestation. Thus, future increases in food production must come primarily from higher yields per unit of land rather than from land expansion.

Agricultural research has successfully developed yield-enhancing technology for the majority of crops grown in temperate zones and for several crops grown in tropical zones. The dramatic impact of agricultural research and modern technology on wheat and rice yields in Asia and Latin American since the mid-1980s is well-known. Less dramatic but significant yield gains have been obtained from research and technological change in other crops, particularly maize.

## Natural Resource Management and Environmental Considerations

Research, technology development, incentives, and regulations are needed to prevent environmental degradation. These measures include appropriate water management policies, reduction of subsidies that encourage wasteful use of inputs better definition of ownership and user rights to resources including land, education of farmers to encourage appropriate use of technology and resource conservation, and the provision of alternatives to resource-degrading inputs and techniques. Since poverty is a major source of degradation, poverty eradication is justified also on environmental grounds.

The recent surge in public and private concerns about negative environmental effects of economic growth and development may, if sustained, have important implications for agricultural development and future food production and consumption. Of particular concern of the need to avoid degradation of natural resources such as land and water, as well as deforestation, water contamination, and health risks associated with the use of chemicals. Since most of the current and potential resource degradation and environmental contamination result from situations in which those who cause and possibly benefit from degradation do not pay the costs, neither the market nor the individual producers and consumers are likely to incorporate preventive measures into their behaviour. Only when sufficient damage has been done to influence significantly current or future production costs will market and producer behaviour change. The state is more likely to undertake preventive measures either through publicly funded research and technology development or through incentive policies and regulations. Extensive water logging, salination, and associated land degradation and productivity losses resulting from inappropriate water management are of particular concern in large parts of Asia.

**No Time for Complacency**

Population growth will outstrip growth in food production in Sub-Saharan Africa for a long time to come unless more is done to accelerate agricultural growth. Between now and 2000, the population will grow at more than 3 per cent a year, while food production is likely to grow at 2 per cent or less a year. By the year 2000, the production shortfall is estimated to increase to about 50 million tons of grain equivalent, up from the current level of about 14 million tons. The region will not have the necessary foreign exchange to import such large amounts of food. And African governments will not be able to count on enough food aid to make up the difference. If current trends continue, by the year 2020, Africa will have a food shortage of 250 million tons, which is more than 20 times the current food gap.

Poverty is expected to increase rapidly in the coming years. Sub-Saharan Africa's share of the world's poor is expected to increase from the current 19 per cent to about 28 per cent in 2000. Furthermore, the number of underweight children is expected to increase in the 1990's in Sub-Saharan Africa.

Asian demand for cereals is estimated to grow at an annual rate of 2.1 per cent between now and the year 2000, whereas food production is expected to grow at 1.9 per cent per year. Much of the production shortfall is likely to be dealt with through expanded imports and perhaps through expanded regional production in response to price increases.

In Latin America, by contrast, growth in food production is anticipated to exceed food demand growth: food production is estimated to grow by 3 per cent annually between 1990 and 2000, while food demand is estimated to grow by 2.5 per cent per year.

Large areas of land are rapidly being degraded and deforested. And the principal reasons for environmental degradation—poverty, high population growth, and limited access to appropriate agricultural technology—are not being dealt with effectively.

About 700 million people are food insecure for them the food crisis has arrived. For the 10-12 million pre-school children who died in 1994 from hunger and diseases related to malnutrition, the food crisis came and went. One-third of the pre-school children of the Third World are unable to grow to their full potential and face increased risk of death and disease.

Complacency is not in order. Clearly, Malthus underestimated the power of science to expand food production. The mass starvation that was predicted for Asia in the 1970s and 1980s did not occur because science was effectively put to work to expand crop·yields. However, past yield increases came about people with foresight made appropriate decisions. The failure to expand investments in agricultural research and technology development during the 1980s and 1990s indicates that such foresight no longer prevails. Given the long lag time between investment in agricultural research and the resulting production increases, failure to invest today will show up in production shortfalls 10 to 20 years from now. The problems associated with environmental degradation will present themselves sooner. We must not wait until a global food crisis is upon us or until the last tree has fallen to make these investments.

## REFERENCES

1. FAO, *FAO Production Yearbook.*
2. FAO, *The State of Food and Agriculture* 1992.
3. FAO, *Agriculture Towards,* 2010.

4. FAO, *The State of Food and Agriculture,* 1994.

5. FAO, *Food Outlook* (December 1994).

6. World Bank, *World Development Report,* 1995.

7. World Bank, *Global Economic Prospects and the Developing Countries.*

8. World Food Programme, *Food Aid in Review* (Rome, WFP 1992).

9. World Bank, *Global Economic Prospects and the Developing Countries,* 1992. (Washington, D.C.: World Bank).

# Chapter 13

## Health Care Relief in Conflict Situations

### *What Can We Learn from the Food Relief Experience?*

Conflicts and war occur in many of the poorest nations where populations already suffer from severe ill-health. War leads to an increase in disease and to a worsening of the already fragile condition of populations. Health care itself becomes a victim of conflict. Many deaths which occur during these emergencies are not discretely related to the conflict itself but are the result of lacking access to public health services. Furthermore, conflict itself but are the result of lacking access to public health services. Furthermore, conflict contributes to the deterioration of already pre-existing structural weaknesses of the health care system. An example is the period of internal conflict in Uganda (1970-86) when health services declined in the aftermath of the war due to the impact of foreign assistance and the planning vacuum in which the activities took place.

#### The Impact of Conflict on Health Care

Conflict and civil strife may lead to a major disruption of health services. This is not only a result of physical destruction but also of finding shortages since national governments increase spending on military activities. Casualties increase the demand for curative services which can divert already limited resources from preventive care.

In the case of the Sudanese civil war a large majority of health professionals were forced to abandon rural health services and left for urban areas or neighbouring countries in order to find new employment. Entire preventive health services such as immunisation as well as water and sanitation projects collapsed leaving the population exposed to infectious diseases and epidemics. In urban areas, the gap in public health care provision is sometimes filled with the expansion of private services. In rural areas, private sector involvement in health care is rather marginal, apart from some omission hospitals or pharmacies. Therefore the non-formal health care sector often makes a substantial contribution towards health care.

With the rise of internal conflicts in Africa, more people suffer from emergency situations. This also increases the influence and impact of international donors. External assistance now a days accounts for more than 25 per cent of government health expenditure in Sub-Saharan Africa.

The size of donor involvement reflects the power of international agencies to control the policy domain. Countries in conflict or post-conflict situations are under pressure to 'rescue' their health systems and accept global policies in exchange for aid assistance and relief.

However, in the period after 1991, donor organisations tended to increase their expenditures for high profile humanitarian operations rather than ordinary development activities. This shift may reflect the increasing influence of media covering some of the conflicts. Too often, organisations intervene with ad hoc assistance without sufficient consultation at local level.

**Donors' Perceptions in Designing Relief Interventions**

Today, in many parts of Sub-Saharan Africa development assistance has virtually collapsed and has been substituted by relief assistance. The problem is that relief interventions are based on a Western construction of reality, reflecting what is desirable and necessary in times of conflict.

Most interventions therefore stress physical and material needs, presuming that the social aspect of food and health is not an immediate issue to address.

The question which arises here is on who's views and perceptions these needs are based? While donors interest may be guided from the perspective of ill-health, the recipient government may be concerned with the collapse of the economy. However, any intervention needs to take into account that local knowledge and practices are shaped by state interests as well as power relationships. The common belief that health care systems always collapse due to conflict is sometimes mistaken. Considering the fact that today's internal conflicts are often fragmented, conflicts do not necessarily result in a breakdown of the health care delivery system.

Donors tend to respond with a 'package' approach and developing countries ministries of health increasingly play a symbolic role. The evidence suggests that international organisations tend to create vertical programmes which undermine national public health programmes. Foreign interventions are technically sophisticated and reorienting health are towards a more curative approach. Too little attentions given to strengthen the health care system within its own limits, providing more appropriate technology, drugs and emphasizing the training of local health staff.

Another vital issue concerns the existence of already fragile health information systems. Agencies tend to bring their own systems which leads to further fragmentation. The local perspective on what are the 'basic needs' in physical and social health are usually not considered. Health relief interventions do not recognize the potential of the communities and the non-formal health sector such as healers and traditional midwifes in supporting and maintaining health care sector presents a substantial contribution towards health. It is not the question between choosing either allopathic or traditional services, it is more the decision which kind of illness will be best treated by which practitioner.

There is a need in further exploring the role of this sector particularly since this is sometimes the only service available for certain populations.

**Responding to Local Needs**

More community-based public health interventions could be vital to reduce mortality and morbidity. For example, in Somalia during the 1992 war and famine high mortality rates due to measles and diarrhoea could has been prevented by involving the communities in primary health care activities such as immunisation and nutrition improvement.

In the African context Tigray is an example where health services had been sustained and partially expanded during the civil war against the Ethiopian government. Local government structures called Baitos promoting social and economic development. Baitos encouraged communities to establish revolving funds for drugs and medical equipment. It actually functioned as an early type of community financing system.

As mentioned above, the challenge in changing health care relief strategies is to overcome the approach of short-term interventions, particularly in a changing conflict environment where conflicts are complex and interruptions are no longer short-term. Therefore interventions need to be linked with the process of conflict resolution to avoid health care or food aid being used by politically dominant groups.

**Food Relief in Conflict Situations**

Food interventions have both a survival and a production function. For example, food-for-work may be part of an income programme or food aid can be monetised to generate local currency. However, food aids have to be seen beyond the objective to fulfill nutritional goals, it also defines relationships between social groups in regard to food accessibility and how food is shared. Food aid is aiming to meet people's basic food requirements and minimising risk and severity of disease by complementing services such as basic health care.

In more stable political conditions where free food aid is given it presents an income transfer by releasing income, which normally is spent on food. However, in conflict situations food relief frequently becomes part of the dynamics of conflict such as in the case of Sudan where it is used to sustain the struggle between the North and the South without resolving it. Furthermore, the military attack food supplies in the fight against rebels who depend on the support from the communities.

Health is also a matter of food security. When food insecurity coincides with conflict situations, health and survival are threatened. Food security provided some concepts on how and why vulnerable households manage to survive in periods of hardship (coping strategies).

**Coping Strategies in African Trouble Zones**

Today, most conflicts in Africa such as the ones in the Great Lake Region, Angola or Congo cause major problems of food insecurity. They are linked to the civil wars which produce substantial social disruption as a result of massive population movements. The analysis of coping strategies showed that household respond to these conflict situation by eating less, selling livestock and land, or trying to find new sources of income.

In some emergency situations, however, such coping mechanisms may fall. In the case of the war in Mozambique food aid was vital since coping strategies were limited and people had to sell all their assets which was particular true for internationally displaced persons and refugees.

It has been argued that food relief bypasses local structures in favour of those qualifying on a nutrition status criterion, decided by international organisations, or it may attract populations to refugee camps to receive free food rations and thereby undermines local production. In the case of Rwanda food aid was targeted at the internally displaced and left out the local population. This can be due to donor bias in needs assessment.

Food scarcity is not always so result of civil war but its creation may be rather a political objective. An example is food relief manipulated by local elites and the military like in the case of Sudan. It can be summarised that generally relief operations often bear the risk of fueling the process of instability and violence rather than helping to contain the situation.

**Lessons from Food Relief for the Health Sector**

Through the experience of food relief in recent civil wars such as Sudan, Somalia, Mozambique etc., there has been an increasing awareness of the economic and political context in which operations takes place. Like food relief, health care is a political tool, which can, if not properly targeted, undermine peoples access to health care services. While food production is linked to food security, it is more difficult to identify factors leading to self-sufficiency in health care.

As mentioned above, food aid is aiming to insure survival. It also has an economic aspect, protecting household assets. Health care relief is targeted to assure immediate physical survival based on the importance of social health. Unfortunately, curative interventions hardly consider the socio-cultural dimension of health. Therefore it would be beneficial if health care interventions consider local norms and traditions. Interventions should be compatible and complement local health programmes. The emphasis should be on strengthening formal and non-formal health institutions both in service provision and training.

In food relief, distribution and needs assessment identification are controversial issues for discussion. While the programme design is shaped by donors' perceptions, the actual programmes are influenced by the priorities of some powerful leaders as well as the socio-economic and political context.

Health care interventions need to analyse these issues in the context of economic and political systems in order to identify the most vulnerable groups, for example populations living in areas which are more, operations require a stronger involvement of communities both as users and active participants to carry out and maintain public health programmes.

There is a need for a new concept to be designed which applies to chronic emergencies. In the absence of a policy framework, guidelines need to be developed in order to overcome the inconsistency in planning and implementation. Donors need to change their assumptions on which they plan their health relief responses. A starting point in improving the efficiency of these operations is to provide institutional support to local authorities and organisations and involve them in the planning and implementation of programmes.

# Chapter 14

## Genetic Diversity and Food Security

Maintaining a diversity of crops and varieties is a key to survival for millions of farmers living on impoverished land. For thousands of years, farmers have used the genetic variation in wild and cultivated plants to develop their crops and raise new breeds of livestock. Genetic diversity gives species the ability to adapt to changing environments, including new pests and diseases and new climatic conditions. Plant genetic resources—that component of genetic diversity of actual or potential use to humanity—provide the raw material for breeding new varieties of crops. These, in turn, provide a basis for more productive and resilient production systems that are better able to cope with such stresses as drought or overgrasing and can reduce the potential for soil erosion. The use of genetic diversity—on-farm, through field experimentation or in sophisticated gene transfer procedures—remains arguably the best route so securing our food and that of our children.

Although science has made enormous strides in improving the world's ability to feed itself over the past three decades, we cannot afford to rest idle. Nearly 800 million people in the developing world do not have enough to eat. In these regions, the rural poor represent about 73 per cent of the people living in poverty. They often live in marginal or unsuitable farming areas, such as zones with saline soils, and conditions, or degraded or hilly areas. Often isolated from other farms and far from urban areas, many poor farmers have barely benefited from agricultural developments elsewhere. In many cases they do no have access to commercially bred high yielding crop varieties. Diversity flourishes and remains important under such conditions.

**Selections and Breeding**

Poor farmers are well aware of the relationship between the stability and sustainability of crops and crop varieties on their lands. Their management and use of a diverse range of plants has often helped them to survive under the most difficult conditions. By growing a range of different crops, farmers have a better chance of meeting their needs. These might be crops that mature at different times or that can be easily stored to help to ensure a stable food supply throughout the year. They may also help farmers provide a nutritionally balance diet for their families, exploit different environment niches that exist on their land, or diversity their income sources.

Importantly, the genetic diversity contained in different varieties provides farmers with options to develop, through selection and breeding, new and more productive crops that are resistant to pests and diseases. The result may be a vast range of local varieties of crops grown by farmers in any one area.

Not respecting diversity can incur high costs: in 18th century Ireland, where potatoes were the only significant source of food for about one-third of the population, farmers came to rely almost entirely on one very fertile and productive variety, which proved susceptible to the devastating potato blight fungus. The resulting famine caused the death or emigration of more than 20 per cent of the population.

The value of diversity goes well beyond its ability to support stable production systems in marginal environments. As the world's human popualtion rises, environmental problems (desertification, deforestation, erosion etc.) are intensifying, climate change, particularly global warming, could bring about drastic changes in the location of the world's agro-ecological zones. Farmers will require new crop varieties capable of producing under diverse conditions, without adding ever-increasing amounts of fertilisers and other agro-chemicals. Because of the limited scope for growth in the world's cultivated areas, each new generation of varieties will have to be more productive than its predecessors.

Much has been written about the use of genetic engineering in plant breeding. Modern molecular techniques can be used to transfer genes from one living organism to another or to change the genetic material within to produce more desirable traits. Genetic Engineering has enormous potential to help solve problems that have proved intractable using conventional breeding approaches, such as developing crop varieties with in-built resistance to keep pests and diseases and tolerance to stresses such as drought. However, the possible impact of these techniques, particularly on human health and the environment, is giving rise to fierce worldwide debate.

Take the case of banana and its close relative plantain, two of the developing world's most important crops. Their improvement is hindered by the sterility of most cultivars, a problem that can be addressed through genetic engineering. It is now possible to transfer gene constructs, such as those associated with disease resistance, directly into varieties with other desirable characteristics, drastically reducing the need for pesticides.

Today, research on genetic engineering is focussed on the development of commercial varieties of the world's major crops of interest to industrialised farmers. Many of the staple crops of importance to poor farmers in developing countries, such as cassava, bananas, beans and yams, have received relatively little attention. This situation is likely to continue as plant breeding is increasingly privatised and biotechnology becomes the fast-growing province of private industry. Meanwhile, the high costs of the new technologies are quickly exceeding the capacity of many, if not most, public research institutions—both in developing and developed countries—to support them. Thus, for the time being, increasing agriculture's role in the development of the world's poor is likely to continue to depend on the identification, maintenance and use of genetic diversity.

# Chapter 15

## Assessing the Costs, Benefits and Risks of GM Crops

Opponents of genetic engineering in agriculture consider it the work of the devil, claiming it harbours untold ecological risks and health hazards and make farmers worldwide dependent on a small number of seed producers. Its advocates, however, see genetically modified crops as a way out of poverty, a unique opportunity to produce enough food for the world's growing population. This paper tries to assess the pros and cons of GM crops case-by-case. The world's farmers already produce enough food to meet global needs and that hunger is due largely to patch patterns of food distribution and lack of purchasing power. The task of tackling distribution problems, however, needs to be flanked by action designed to improve farmers ability to achieve higher yields from their land—so they can feed themselves and others through their own efforts. If genetic engineering can help them do so and where it compares favourably to other options, so the use of GM plants should not be hindered.

If you look at the opportunities and risks GM might present for agriculture in developing countries. Pest-resistant Bt cotton, for example, has led to a marked upturn in yields in China and South Africa. In the South Africa province of Kwazulu/Natal, where the average farm is around 1.7 hectares small, the percentage of farmers who switched to genetically modified cotton from 1999 to 2002 jumped from 12 per cent to an estimated 95 per cent. One of the problems as sociated with Bt cotton is that 90 per cent of the biotech are held by a single enterprise—the Monsanto Group based in the USA. What's more, there are signs that resistance to cotton pests leads to an increase in other pests, which then need to be fought using more pesticides.

Taking a look at herbicide-resistant soya beans, the need to weigh up GM's pros and cons on a case by case basis. Herbicide resistance makes manual weeding unnecessary—which may be a handicap where desperately needed jobs could be lost. But where agriculture suffers from a growing shortage of labour—as it does in southern Africa due to AIDS-less labour—intensive crops could be a boon. However, in so-called "diversity centers" (region where many different varieties of a specific plant are grown) - such as Mexico (for maize) or India (for cotton)—the risk of non-GM crops being contained by air-borne pollen needs to be taken particularly seriously.

Among the prime requirements for the use of GM in agriculture are effective monitoring. Before introducing GM crops, the benefits and risks need to be carefully assessed. And after a permit is granted, care must be taken to ensure that farmers can buy seed at fair prices and have access to advice. In most developing countries, however, state institutions capable of providing such guarantees are few and far between. Such bodies need to be created, with the help of international development cooperation. In addition, developing countries have to cooperate more extensively at regional levels, for instance by sharing environmental impact assessments. The biotech companies operating in developing countries are called upon to involve small-scale farmers In their plant breeding operations so they can take greater account of their needs and preferences.

## Chapter 16

# GMOs and the Politics of International Trade

Ever since it was announced in 1999, the most prominent nexus linking these two fields has been the European Union's de facto moratorium on new approvals for the politics of biotechnology are often played out through the politics of international trade, production and import of GMOs. The moratorium continues to fuel a heated trade dispute between the United States and the EU. The dispute has major implications not only for these two trading partners, but also for the global politics of biotechnology in agriculture and trade.

The US and the EU are major trading partners, aid donors and providers of foreign direct investment for many developing countries. The size of the European and North American markets means that they strongly affect global food and feed production and commodity prices. For these reasons, among others, their policies and decisions on biotechnology and agricultural trade affect the policies of many other countries. Among the immediate impacts of the EU moratorium have been

- A rapid switch by European buyers of commodities like soya beans and maize, from North American suppliers to those in countries that are formally GM—free such as Brazil. This has contributed to a dramatic change in the flows of transatlantic trade.

- A significant slow-down in the Chinese commercialization of GM food crops. China appeared poised to commercialise GM varieties of food crops such as rice and maize. Quite suddenly, the commercialization of GM food crops was—unofficially—put on hold, although China continued to commercialise varieties of transgenic insect-resistant cotton. India has behaved in a similar way.
- A new fragmentation in the politics of biotechnology among farmers and industry groups in North America. Whereas transgenic crops such as soyabean, maize, cotton and canola had been commercialized with remarkably little fuss, wheat growers and food processors in the US have called for biotechnology corporations to delay commercializing transgenic wheat until consumer acceptance in export markets has been secured.

**Achieving Acceptance by the Back Door?**

The United States, backed by other countries and transnational corporations, argues that restrictions on trade in GMOs amount to an unwarranted restriction on trade that contravenes WTO rules, distorts world markets, and prevents consumers from having the opportunity to choose GM foods. Nevertheless, European consumers continue to exhibit serious misgivings about GMOs. Biotechnology industry representatives acknowledge that an attempt by the US to use the WTO to force open European markets to GMOs would be resented by many people and could be disastrous for consumer acceptance in Europe.

The export of American GM food aid to famine affected countries in southern Africa has also provoked suspicion that the US government is attempting to achieve acceptance of GMOs by the back door. In a series of extraordinary public diatribes, senior US officials have used the controversy to attack both African and European leaders, arguing that it is more important to feed starving people than worry about the 'irrational' concerns of well-fed Europeans. However, African governments have justifiable concerns about both biosafety and protecting their future trading relations with important export markets in Europe. This episode has provoked increased suspicion that the US is willing to use its diplomatic and economic weight to make the international spread of GMOs a *fait accompli*.

The Biosafety Protocol, governing the transboundary movement of GMOs, will shortly enter into force. The protocol recognizes that GMOs may pose different risks in different environments, and requires the implementation of effective mechanisms for risk assessment of GMOs at the national level before they may be imported. Many developing countries are at an early stage of elaborating their legal frameworks and face a difficult challenge in building their capacity to enforce them. They need time and the support of richer countries to complete this task.

However, although 103 countries have signed the protocol, the US is not a Parry. American exports of GM food aid to countries which have not yet implemented their biosafety management regimes seem calculated to preempt and undermine the protocol. Its willingness to use the threat of a WTO dispute to gain entry to European markets suggests that it is determined to subordinate the protocol to international 'free trade' rules.

**Closing Down Options for Diversification?**

Many producers in the developed and developing world are examining the potential of diversifying production in order to exploit multiple markets, which may include GM, organic and 'GM-free' products. However, there is significant uncertainty on the question of whether GM and non-GM crops can be effectively segregated to a level that will be acceptable to consumers. Existing organic producers and consumers are angry about the potential threat posed to their markets and freedom of choice by the risk of gene flow between GM and other crops.

Advocates of biotechnology, such as the American Soyabean Association, argue vociferously that segregation will be prohibitively expensive, if not technically impossible to achieve under all but the most liberal thresholds. Research suggests that coexistence of GM and non-GM agriculture may be possible, at a regional level, for particular crops and particular farm-types. However, it would demand significant changes in farming practices for some crops and could impose significant additional costs. A very low level of contamination (0.1%) will be extremely difficult, if not practically impossible, to achieve for all the crops and farm types considered. Segregation is particularly unlikely in small-holder farming systems in developing countries.

**Risks and Opportunities for Developing Countries**

Some developing countries are vulnerable to the risks of losing markets in the EU through GM contamination. In Namibia, for example, where approximately 80 per cent of the country's meat exports go to the EU, livestock farmers are concerned that GM animal feed entering the country unofficially could undermine the confidence of European consumers. Similarly, the recent controversy over GM food aid shipments to famine-affected southern African countries was heightened by fears among the recipients countries that GM grain, if planted, could threaten exports to the EU. Such fears contributed to Zambia's decision to refuse the food aid altogether, while Malawi, Mozambique and Zimbabwe agreed to accept the shipments on condition that they were milled to prevent planting.

Other developing countries, such as Brazil, may feel that they can take advantage of the difficulties faced by American producers and shippers in meeting the European demand for non-GM supplied of crops such as soyabeans. Ironically, it is widely acknowledged that GM seeds are being grown in parts of Brazil, which presents a risk to the country's exporters because European processors and supermarkets have the power to impose stringent standards of purity on suppliers, and can reject shipments.

Some developing countries may be relatively insulated from the effects of the EU-US tussle. For example, China and India both have large domestic markets which may enable them to commercialise certain GM crops without threatening exports. A recent analysis of GM commercialization scenarios in China argues that the country could realize significant gains domestically from commercializing some GM crops, regardless of the policies adopted by potential export markets.

# Chapter 17

## Intellectual Property Rights, Biotechnology and Development

Developing countries are being urged to implement strong intellectual property rights (IPRs) in order to enable poor farmers to take advantage of genetically modified crops. IPRs are claimed to provide a vital stimulus for trade, investment, innovation and technology transfer for development. However, for many developing countries, the costs of implementing IPR regimes outweigh the benefits and may even undermine development in the long term. IPRs do little to stimulate private research into crops and traits of importance to food security in poor countries, and tend to hamper public research that could address these needs.

Biotechnology companies argue that IPRs provide a vital incentive for investment in expensive biotechnological research and development, and provide the necessary safeguards to encourage them to commercialise their genetically engineered products in developing countries. Largely in response to industry pressure, harmonized standards of IPR protection have been agreed at the global level, chiefly through the World Trade Organisation's (WTO) Agreement on Trade Related intellectual Property Rights (TRIPs), which requires developing countries to implement strong domestic IPR regimes.

Influential voices in international agricultural research and policy networks have also urged developing countries to implement TRIPs as part of a suite of enabling policies to promote agricultural biotechnology. However, claims that IPRs are essential prerequisites for innovation in, and technology transfer to, developing countries do not stand up to close scrutiny.

A recent study, by the independent UK Commission on Intellectual Property Rights (CIPR), confirms that IPRs may benefit those developing countries that already possess a fairly high level of manufacturing and innovation capacity, but bring few benefits for the poor. For the poorest countries, the costs of strong IPRs outweigh the benefits in the short term, and potentially in the long term as well.

IPRs do little to stimulate investment where there is no likely lucrative market for the end product. Thus, while IPRs may succeed in generating private investor interest in cash crops produced in developing countries, they are not effective in stimulating investment in subsistence crops and traits relevant to poor farmers or food security. In addition, patents may restrict farmers' conventional rights to save and exchange seeds. The experiences of some North American farmers, who have been sued by biotech firms for breaching their contracts and infringing company patents, vividly testifies to this likelihood.

The CIPR recommends that developing countries should tailor their IPR regimes to their national circumstances and developmental priorities, taking full advantage of the flexibility the TRIPs Agreement allows. Among other recommendations, they are advised to

- Exclude plants and animals from patent protection;
- Explicitly allow farmers to save, reuse and possibly even sell and exchange harvested seeds;
- Allow access to protected varieties for further research and breeding; and

- Resist further attempts in international fora to entrench a global, 'one-sizefits-all' IPRs standard.

However, few developing countries appear to be following this approach. For some, the reasons may be associated with a lack of expertise, leading to a lack of awareness about the available options and the possible advantages of using them. Such countries tend to be the ones most reliant on multilateral, bilateral and even private 'capacity-building' support, which generally promotes strong IPRs models. In addition, many developing countries have foregone TRIPs flexibilities in order to preserve key bilateral trade, aid and investment relationships with wealthy countries, which support stronger IPRs.

Larger and economically more powerful developing countries like India have been more creative in developing IPRs legislation that is tailored to their needs, including provisions allowing farmers to save, use, resow, exchange, share and even sell their seeds. However, such 'sui generis' solutions are likely to be challenged by industry and it remains to be seen whether they will survive judicial scrutiny. In developed countries, courts and patent offices have generally interpreted intellectual property laws in a manner that supports the biotechnology industry's demands for strong IPRs. At the international level, sui generic IPRs regimes may be vulnerable to legal challenges through the WTO, which is ill-equipped to reconcile trade objectives with socio-economic and environmental considerations.

**Policy Responses**

The policy consensus—that strong IPRs are good for development—seems to be entrenched. Nevertheless, it is coming under increasing scrutiny, and perhaps the criticisms and recommendations for reform will be heeded. However, the political willingness to acknowledge its flaws, and to take on its champions, is conspicuously absent. So long as this situation continues, the result is likely to be the further entrenchment of technological inequality and the

**undermining of development in the long-term. In order to avoid this undesirable outcome, the following policy responses need to be considered urgently**

- Greater scrutiny of the developmental effects of IPRs, particularly the linkages with poverty and food security
- In particular, attention needs to be paid to the impacts of strong IPRs on public good research, especially the tendency for patent rights to inhibit the exchange of knowledge and technology and divert scarce resources away from frontline research.
- Proposals for reform of the TRIPs regime, currently under consideration, should preserve the rights of WTO member to tailor their IPRs regimes according to their particular circumstances, especially with regard to the special needs of poor farmers.
- Multilateral and bilateral donors, international and philanthropic organizations should provide effective support to developing countries to design and implement IPRs laws that support their developmental priorities.

**Thickets of Patents**

Scientific innovations build on existing knowledge that has accrued over generations. IPRs allow innovators to claim exclusive rewards for each incremental step they have contributed. When genetic engineering is applied to plants, successive layers of IPRs accumulate over the plant material itself, as novel varieties with desirable traits are used as the basis for further R&D. The rapid accumulation of IPRs over germless and enabling technologies has caused a rapid increase in transaction costs, as IP owners have to be identified, licenses negotiated or disputes litigated.

This has led to a number of consequences for the biotechnology sector, with implications for the conduct of agricultural research of relevance to developing countries, including:

- Dramatic consolidation among biotech firms, keen to avoid lengthy negotiations for technology licenses and/ or patent litigation.
- Hampering the exchange of data, plant material and enabling technologies among researchers in both public and private sectors.
- Increasing the costs of administering the IPR system, as patent offices have been inundated with applications from firms and universities seeking to build a 'defensive' patent portfolio.

The private sector has responded to the 'IPR thicket problem' by buying access to as wide a portfolio of patents as possible. Solution for public sector researchers, in both developed and developing countries, are more difficult to find. The idea of a common pool or clearing house of publicly-owned IP is being seriously considered in influential policy circles, aimed at facilitating the protection, transfer and even commercial exploitation of public IP. This apparently pragmatic approach brings its own legal, administrative and political difficulties, with cost implications. In particular, it requires public-sector research institutions to expend their scarce resources on developing their IPR-management capacity.

# Chapter 18

## Corporate Dominance and Agricultural Biotechnology
### *Implications for Development*

The development and commercialization of agricultural biotechnology has profound implications for developing countries and poof farmers, whether or not they have access to it. Contrary to the enthusiastic claims of some of biotechnology's cheerleaders, these are likely to include adverse as well as beneficial consequence for those who depend on farming. But biotechnology's evolution will be driven largely by the decisions of company directors and research scientists in the private sector, who are preoccupied with corporate profitability and competitiveness, rather than the problems of poverty, food security and economic development in poor countries.

A genetically modified crop which requiresless labour for its cultivation might benefit the landowning poor, but would undermine the livelihoods of landless people who rely on income from agricultural labour. Similarly, genetic engineering may be used to develop novel crop varieties which could undermine developing countries' export markets. An example is the attempt by an American company to engineer a new variety of rice, based on a Thai variety, that will grow in Florida. In this fashion, the application of agricultural biotechnology can have positive and negative developmental impacts. However, these consequences are not intrinsic to biotechnology. The actual effects will be determined by the way the technology is applied in practice.

**Private Sector Dominance**

The private sector is currently in a better position than the public sector to mobilize the major resources necessary to carry out sophisticated biotechnology research. Consequently, the decisions of private companies will largely determine what R&D takes place and which products are commercialized, even though most biotechnology research in developing countries involves the public sector. In this respect, private sector decision-makers probably have more influence over the developmental impact of agricultural biotechnology than their counterparts in the public sector, whether they be in government, agricultural research institutes or even the major multilateral, bilateral and philanthropic donor agencies.

Budgets in the public agricultural research sector are under great pressure. At the same time, public sector researchers' 'freedom to operate' is undermined by a battery of legal instruments (intellectual property rights, research contracts, material transfer agreements and so on), that impose extra transaction costs. For the private sector, these costs represent important investments to safeguard future income and preserve key commercial assets, but for the public sector they are a burden on their financial and technical resources, and inhibit their traditional strengths in working collaboratively to generate public goods.

The crops and traits commercialized so far have been targeted at the needs of large-scale commercial farmers, particularly in North America. Even observers who are favourable towards biotechnology universally agree that the crops, traits and challenges of interest to poor farmers in developing countries are being neglected. Critics point out that the tendency of both private and public sectors to focus on GM distracts attention from research into alternative technologies including advanced non-transgenic biotechnologies—that are more likely to be appropriate to the capacity of both science institutes and farmers in developing countries.

**The Private Sector and Public 'Developmental' Goods**

There is a shortfall in R&D directed at the production of 'public goods' for development. The public sector is poorly positioned to address this gap. For their part, the major biotechnology firms have embarked on a few projects designed to demonstrate the capacity of biotechnology to contribute to development.

The private sector's willingness to engage with projects like vitamin-A rice, virus-resistant sweet-potato and the Insect-Resistant Maize for Africa (IRMA) project should perhaps be welcomed. But the rarity and small scale of such projects only serves to highlight the yawning gap between them and the array of crops and traits already commercialized for developed country markets.

Projects like vitamin-A rice and IRMA seem to happen against the odds, in the particular circumstances when public or philanthropic circumstances can agree terms with the private sector. Although company executives are often willing in principle to engage with such initiatives, in practice they will only do so under very particular conditions, which include strict safeguards for their intellectual property rights. Ultimately, the decision to get involved hinges on a hard-headed business assessment about whether the philanthropic or public endeavour may undermine the company's commercial interests.

For example, Monsanto's willingness to share its rice data certainly helped public researchers to complete the sequencing of the rice genome more quickly. However, the agreement came with strict conditions on who could use the information, and how. Significantly, it happened when the company had decided to direct its R&D efforts away from rice to concentrate on four other crops.

Much more profound and far-reaching than any philanthropic project or public-private partnership, the impact of corporate strategies in the developing world will be felt through their core business activities. As things stand, the public sector is poorly-equipped to address the needs of poor farmers, and companies will continue to concentrate on high-value proprietary GM technologies, attuned to the needs of wealthy markets in developed countries. There is a risk than small-holders in developing countries will be left to apply spin-off technologies, in the hope that crops developed with the agronomic and economic conditions of developed countries in mind, will nevertheless perform acceptably well under their own conditions.

Corporate voluntarism can only achieve a small amount of good in terms of harnessing appropriate and socially desirable biotechnology for development. Therefore, an effective, coherent regime of public policy and regulation is urgently needed. This should include:

- Public funding for R&D to address the need of developing country farmers for affordable, appropriate technologies.
- A regulatory framework to ensure that the core business activities of companies will contribute to development rather than undermine it. This may entail
    1. Providing incentives for companies to develop products for which large markets do not exist;
    2. Re-examining the scope of IPRs to ensure that undesirable monopolies are not created and public-good research is not inhibited.
    3. The effective enforcement of competition and anti-trust laws in order to tackle the negative consequences of concentration in the biotech and seed sectors; and
    4. A careful evaluation of the potential for policy and regulatory frameworks to create incentives and

institutionalize the best practices of corporate social responsibility and corporate citizenship, in order to harness the capacity of the private sector to deliver public as well as private goods more effectively and more often.

**Business and Biotechnology**

Private companies' commercialization strategies prioritise transgenic crops over other potential biotechnological applications. Genetic engineering is attractive to firms because the ability to register exclusive ownership over new varieties makes it more feasible for them to recoup the high costs of biotech R&D in principle, GM crops have the potential to address key problems relevant to food security and poverty in developing countries. However, in practice the GM seeds commercialized to date by private companies are more expensive than conventional seeds, tend to be marketed along with a package of other inputs such as proprietary chemicals, and have complex management requirements that are often impracticable on small plots of land. Most seriously, they threaten to increase poor farmers' dependence because they restrict their rights to save and exchange seeds.

# Chapter 19

## Population Growth and Grain Production

The relationship between the growth in world population and the grain harvest has shifted over the last half-century, neatly dividing this period into two distinct eras. From 1950 to 1984, growth and the grain harvest easily exceeded that of population, raising the harvest per person from 247 kilograms to 342, a gain of 38 per cent. During the 14 years since then, growth in the grain harvest has fallen behind that of population, dropping output per person from its historic high in 1984 to an estimated 317 kilograms in 1998—a decline of 7 per cent, or 0.5 per cent a year.

These global trends conceal widely divergent developments among countries, contrasts that can be seen for the world's two most populous nations: India and China. In both, grain production per person was close to 200 kilograms as recently as 1978. Since then, the figure in India has edged up slightly but still falls short of 200 kilograms, while in China production has surged since the economic reforms in 1978, with per person output now at nearly 300 kilograms. The combination of a dramatic surge in grain production and an equally dramatic reduction in population growth has given China a large margin of safety, effectively eliminating most of its hunger and malnutrition. Meanwhile, although India has also achieved impressive gains in its harvest, these have been largely cancelled by population growth, leaving its 976 million people living close to the margin.

What has happened in China and India is the story of developing countries in general. The overwhelming majority have achieved substantial, if not dramatic, gains in their grain harvests over the last half-century. Some, such as Thailand, have combined this with a much slower growth of population, which means that agricultural gains translate into rising grain production per person. In Pakistan, by contrast, grain production per person climbed steadily for a while, but it peaked in 1981 at 186 kilograms. Since then it has been declining nearly 1 per cent a year. In effect, Pakistan's farmers are losing the battle with population growth.

The slower growth in the world grain harvest since 1984 is due to the lack of new land and to slower growth in irrigation and fertilizer use. Irrigated area per person, after expanding by 4 per cent since then as growth in the irrigated area has fallen behind that of population.

The increase in world fertiliser use has slowed dramatically since 1990, as diminishing returns to the application of additional fertilizer has stabilised use in the United States, Western Europe, and Japan and slowed annual growth in world fertilizer use from 6 per cent between 1950 and 1990 to scarcely 2 per cent in recent years.

Although Malthus was primarily concerned with the additional demand for grain generated by population growth, rising affluence is also playing a role. In a low income country such as India, grain consumption per person is less than 200 kilograms per year and diets are typically dominated by a single starchy staple-rice, for instance. With scarcely a pound of grain available a day per person, nearly all must be consumed directly, leaving little for conversion into animal protein. For the average American, on the other hand, the great bulk of the 800 kilogram daily grain consumption is taken in indirectly in the form of beef, pork, poultry, eggs, milk, cheese, ice cream, and yogurt. At the intermediate level, in a country like Italy, people consume 400 kilograms of grain a day. Future food price stability thus depends on expanding production fast enough to keep up with both population growth and rising affluence.

One question often asked is: How many people can the Earth support? This must be answered with another question, At what level of consumption? If the world grain harvest of 1.87 billion tons were expanded to 2 billion tons in the years ahead, it would support 10 billion Indians or 2.5 billion Americans. To answer the question of how many people the Earth can support, we first have to know the level of consumption we expect to live at.

Now that the frontiers of agricultural settlement have disappeared, future growth in grain production must come almost entirely from raising land productivity. Unfortunately, this is becoming more difficult. After rising at 2.1 per cent a year from 1950 to 1990, the annual increase in rainland productivity dropped to scarcely 1 per cent from 1990 to 1997. The challenge for the world's farmers is to reverse this decline at a time when cropland area per person is shrinking, the amount of irrigation water per person is dropping, and the crop yield response to additional fertilizer use is falling.

# Chapter 20

## Population Growth and Cropland

Since mid-century, global population has grown much faster than the cropland area. The trend is likely to continue in the next century, dropping cropland per person to historically low levels. The ever smaller per capita cropland base will make food self-sufficiency impossible for many countries, and will test the capacity of international markets to meet a growing demand for imported food.

For millennia, farmers satisfied rising food demand by bringing new land under the plow. But by mid-century cropland expansion could no longer meet the food needs of an increasingly populous and prosperous world. The 10,000 year era of steady expansion was over, and a new era began that stressed raising land productivity. As this high-yielding era shows signs of faltering, concern over the shrinking supply of cropland per person looms ever larger.

Since mid-century, grain area—which serves as a proxy for cropland in general—has increased by some 19 per cent, but global population has grown 132 per cent, seven times faster. Largely as a result, grain area per person has fallen by half since 1950, from 0.24 to 0.12 hectares. Assuming that grain area remains constant, grain area per person will fall to 0.07 hectares by 2050. In crowded industrial countries such as Japan, Taiwan, and South Korea, grain area per capita today is smaller than the area of a tennis court.

As grain area per person falls, more and more nations risk losing the capacity to feed themselves. Having already seen per capita grain area shrink by 40-50 per cent between 1960 and 1998, Pakistan, Nigeria, Ethiopia, and Iran can expect a further 60-70 per cent loss by 2050—a conservative projection that assumes no further losses of agricultural land. The result will be four countries with a combined population of more than 1 billion whose grain area per person will be only 300-600 square metres, less than a quarter of the area in 1950.

The historical record suggests that such a small area per person will send a substantial share of a country's people to world markets for their food. Consider the experience of six countries in East Asia whose per capita grain area currently ranges from 200 to 600 square metres per person. Sri Lanka relies on imports for more than a third of its grain, while Japan, Thiwan, South Korea, and Malaysia buy more than 70 per cent of their grain from abroad. North Koera is the only one of the six that does not import heavily (it gets less than 20 per cent of its grain requirements from abroad), but its population is poorly fed-indeed, on the verge of starvation.

The concern is that population growth will push many nations—not just the four fastest-growing ones—below the 600-square metre-threshold in coming decades. In Asia alone, where grain area per person stands at 800 square metres, 16 countries are poised to cross this threshold by 2050, and many of them much sooner. As this process unfolds, the number of people who will turn to foreign markets for their food will likely jump sharply. These countries will find an increasingly tight international grain market, with nations from the Middle East, North Africa, and other regions already buying a third or more of their grain overseas.

In addition to per capita losses, population growth can lead to degradation of cropland, reducing its productivity or even eliminating it from production. As a country's population density increases and good farmland becomes scarce, poor farmers are forced onto ecologically vulnerable land such as hillsides and tropical forest. In the Philippines, for example, hillside agriculture accounted for only 10 per cent of all agricultural land in 1960, but 30 per cent in 1987. Because it is highly erodible, hillside land is easily damaged; worldwide, some 160 million hectares of hillside farmland—11 per cent of cropland—were characterised in 1989 as "severely eroded." Similarly, population pressure can force peasants to overfarm the poor soils of tropical forests. After being cleared and farmed for a few years, these soils typically require fallow period of 20-25 years, but population pressures keep poor farmers on the same land for far longer than the soils can support, cutting fallow periods to just a few years in some areas of tropical Africa and Asia.

Finally, population pressures on a fixed base of land can result in rural landlessness. In Bangladesh, for example, landlessness among rural households rose from 35 per cent in 1960 to 53 per cent in the early 1990s. Interestingly, Bangladesh is regarded as a success in slowing population expansion, as its growth rate declined from 2.8 per cent in the late 1970s to 1.5 per cent in the early 1990s. But its success came too late to prevent the increase in rural landlessness, highlighting the need to work sooner, rather than later, for population stabilisation.

# Chpater 21

## The Uruguay Round Agreement on Agriculture

The Uruguay Round Agreement on Agriculture (URAA) calls for the initiation of negotiations for continuing the process of agricultural trade reform in 1999. Article 20 of the agreement states that member countries of the World Trade Organisation (WTO) recognize that the long-term objective of substantial progressive reductions in trade distorting support and protection of agriculture resulting in fundamental reforms is an ongoing process.

The Uruguay Round Agreement on Agriculture, which entered into force in 1995 along with other Uruguay Round accords, including the agreement to establish the World Trade Organisation, was an important step toward applying multilateral rules and disciplines to global agricultural trade. Most assessments of the agreement hail it as a historic shift in the way agriculture establishes new multilateral trade agreements. The agreement establishes new multilateral rules governing market access, export subsidies and domestic support for agriculture. In terms of future trade liberalisation, its most important provisions may be those requiring the elimination of quantitative trade restrictions and their conversion to bound tariffs. These bound tariffs, even if some of them are extremely high, can provide a starting point for future negotiations of tariff reductions.

**Market Access**

The agreement requires all WTO members to convert non-tariff trade barriers to tariffs and to reduce them by a simple average of 36 per cent over six years (with a minimum tariff reduction per tariff line of 15 per cent). The agreement prohibits the introduction of new non-tariff barriers to trade. Where nontariff barriers restrict imports, the agreement requires that importing countries offer minimum access of usually 3 per cent of consumption rising to 5 per cent over the six-year implementation period for the agreement.

Most assessments of the agreement conclude that it provides little in the way of expanded access for agricultural products. Its importance lies in extending the principle (already applied to trade in industrial products) of protection by bound tariffs to agricultural trade and establishing at least a base for further tariff reductions in future negotiations.

**Export Subsidies**

The agreement requires that export subsidies be reduced by 21 per cent in terms of quantities and by 36 per cent in terms of budgetary outlays by the end of the six-year implementation period. WTO members may continue to use their existing export subsidies within the limits established, but may not introduce any new export subsidies.

**Domestic Support**

The agreement also includes rules and commitments for domestic support. Domestic subsidies are to be cut by 20 per cent from average levels of support aggregated across all commodities for the base period 1986-88. Support reduction commitments are also to be made over the six-year implementation period on the basis of this aggregate measure of support (AMS).

Trade policy experts contend that the rules established for domestic support policies are more important than the reduction commitments required. The agreement defines which domestic policies are permitted ("green box" policies), such as income support provided to farmers independently of participation in production—limiting programmes, advisory services, or domestic food assistance. Policies that are not eligible for the green box are automatically prohibited ("amber box" policies.)

**Sanitary and Phytosanitary Measures**

An agreement on the Application of Sanitary and Phytosanitary (SPS) Measures reaffirms the right of WTO members to adopt and enforce measures that they deem appropriate to protect human, animal, or plant life or health as long as such measures are not applied in an "arbitrary and unjustified" manner. The agreement states that such measures may not be used as disguised barriers to trade. SPS measures may be based on international standards where they exist. WTO members could impose higher standards than those derived from these sources if based on scientific justification and risk assessment. All WTO members agree to recognise the equivalence of different standards that result in a comparable level of SPS protection. Dispute settlement panels should seek advice from relevant international organisations when scientific or technical matters are at issue.

The SPS Agreement, though binding on WTO members, is stated in broad language. Specific will come from interpretation of the agreement and adjudication of Sanitary and Phytosantitary issues in WTO dispute settlement.

**Dispute Settlement**

New and strengthened dispute settlement procedures agreed to as part of the Uruguay Round also apply to disputes that may arise under either the Agreement on Agriculture or the SPS Agreement. An important change in WTO dispute settlement procedures is the elimination of a member's right to veto a dispute panel's decision and effectively block implementation of the panel's recommendations for resolving the dispute. Potentially this strengthens the ability of the WTO to enforce panel judgements. The right of WTO members to negotiate compensation rather than change its challenged policies remains in place, however.

# Chapter 22

## Irrigation Management

### *Facing the Challenge*

Irrigated agriculture is up against an enormous challenge. India's population continues to grow at a tremendous rate. Over the next 10 years, there will be more extra mouths to feed. Water is becoming increasingly scarce for agriculture, with conflicting demands being made on limited supplies by the domestic and industrial sectors. The most attractive irrigation sites have already been exploited. Yet, irrigated agriculture will have to deliver average output increases of at least 3.5 per cent per year if future food demands are to be met in India.

Forty years ago in the 1950s and 1960s, India has worried about its capacity to produce sufficient food to feed its growing population. Episodes of food scarcity were not uncommon. It was dreaded that millions would die of hunger. Then dawned the miracle of the "green revolution". Cereal production increased by leaps and bounds, boosted by expanded irrigation, increased fertilizer application and modern crop varieties. The vigorous response in mobilising financing towards boosting agricultural production paid off.

Given the importance of irrigation to the India's food supply and the vast resources already expanded on irrigation development, it is tragic that the actual performance of irrigation systems is so disappointingly low. In the post-green revolution era, it has become increasingly evident that the performance of irrigation systems, especially large-scale systems, is suboptimal whether measured in terms of achieving planned area targets or in terms of production potentials created by the physical works.

In many irrigation systems, the actual area irrigated is much less than the command area. Sharp inequities in water supplies between farmers in the head reaches of irrigation systems and those located downstream is another manifestation of poor performance. Investigations in the Tungabhadra Irrigation Scheme reveal that the tail-end of a major distributory commanding 25 per cent of the total area, received approximately 20-40 per cent of the targeted discharge while the upper reaches got more than their share.

Lack of maintenance has caused many systems to fall into disrepair, further inhibiting performance. Over time, distribution canals have become silted up, increasing the likelihood of breaching, damage to outlets and leading to salt build-up in the soil.

**Successful Farmer-Managed Irrigation Systems**

Farmers have long demonstrated their potential capability to manage irrigation systems efficiently. Farmer-managed irrigation systems, (FMIS) also known as traditional, indigenous, communal or peoples' systems, are often classified "minor" or "small-scale" irrigation systems, although they may be found in command areas of 15,000-20,000 hectares.

Many successful farmer-managed irrigated systems which have been functioning effectively for hundreds of years, represent a valuable, accumulated investment. They are also reservoirs of largely untapped irrigation management experience.

Research has revealed that FMIS contribute to the production of a significant portion of the subsistence food supply. Ground water irrigation systems, often found in areas affected by drought, play a strategic role in promoting food security. In India ground water development which is increasing in importance is predominantly farmer-managed. In this country an estimated 20 million hectares are already under ground water irrigation. When mismanaged though, ground water irrigation could impact negatively on the environment.

In addition to the hectarage under farmer-managed ground water irrigation, farmer-managed tank irrigation systems cover about 8.5 million hectares in this country. Farmer-managed irrigation systems have also allowed intensification of agriculture to partially meet the food needs of rapidly growing populations.

**Little Awareness**

Yet, despite the widespread interest in irrigation management turnover throughout India there is very little documentation about the processes used and the results obtained from irrigation management turnover. Many policy-makers do not know-how to turn over management of their irrigation institutions in an effective way. They typically have very little, if any, awareness of the range of organisational options which may be suitable under different conditions. There is an urgent need, therefore, for a systematic, comparative assessment of the range of approaches being used, constraints to implementation and the impacts on performance of transferring management to non-governmental or farmers' organisations.

Successful irrigation in the future will be that which supports much higher levels of agricultural productivity, enhances responsiveness to more diversified and dynamic crop markets, stimulates more profitable irrigated agriculture for wide numbers of rural poor, substantially improves water use efficiency and supports the sustainable use of scarce land, biomass and water resources.

In the coming years the irrigation sector will be in ferment, with decision-makers, agency managers and farmers needing better information and strategic processes to make intelligent choices in the management of irrigated agriculture.

# Chapter 23

# A Breakthrough in the Evolution of Large Dams?

### Back to the Negotiating Table

"The problem is not the dams. It is the hunger. It is the thirst. It is the darkness in a township". With these plain words, former South African President Nelson Mandela summed up the World Commission on Dams (WCDs) motives in a speech at the presentation praising its work. His position is similar to that of the many other representatives of the South who were present: he demands a right to development. But Ms Medha Patkar, of India, a WCD Commission member and founder of the Struggle to Save the Narmada River (*Narmada Bachao Andolan*) anti-dam movement, takes a contrary view. "The problems of the dams are only a symptom of the larger failure of the unjust and destructive dominant development model," she says. We need to challenge "the forces that lead to the marginalisation of a majority through the imposition of unjust technologies like large dams".

### Stagnation of Dam Building

The WCD is a unique experiment in reaching consensus. It began in April 1997 when with the support of the World Bank and the World Conversation Union (IUCN), 39 representatives of diverse interests met at a workshop in Gland, Switzerland. At this point the various positions of the participants from governments, the private sector, international financial institutions, civil society organisations and affected people were cast in stone. The Manibeli Declaration in June 1994 of 326 activist groups from 44 countries had called for an immediate moratorium on World Bank funded large dams until a comprehensive, independent review of all Bank funded projects had been conducted. International financial institutions were actually no longer able to fund further large dams in the face of public criticism. Enervated by steadily growing protests despite continual tightening of social and environmental standards, the institutions' representatives wearily likened the dispute to a football match in which somebody kept moving the goalposts. But one proposal to emerge from the meeting in Gland was for all parties to work together in establishing the World Commission on Dams.

The WCD began its work in May 1998 under the chairmanship of Prof. Kader Asmal, then South Africa's Minister of Water Affairs and Forestry. Its 12 members were chosen to reflect regional diversity, expertise and stakeholder perspectives. But the Commission ran the risk of failure right from the start due to their confrontational attitudes. The members, who spent 2 years 6 months jointly organising hearings, consultations and case studies and analysing more than 100 existing large dams, could not be more disparate.

**The Current Situation**

A large dam is a dam with the height of 15 metres or more from the foundation. If dams are 5-15 metres high and have a reservoir volume of more than three million cubic metres, they are also classified as large dams. Using this definition, there are more than 45,000 large dams around the world, almost half of them in China. They were built in the 20th century to meet the constantly growing demand for water and electricity. On a global scale, hydropower dams account for about 20 per cent of electricity generated, and in 24 countries, including Brazil, Democratic Republic of Congo, Zambia and Norway, hydropower covers more than

90 per cent of national electricity supply needs. Half the world's large dams were built solely or mainly for irrigation. Between 12 per cent and 16 per cent of world food production is based on dams, and as reservoirs they provide protection against floods.

Unfortunately, this impressive balance is counteracted by comparably significant problems. Construction of large dams is a major intervention in the ecosystem of rivers and the lives of many people. The WCD estimates that some 40-80 million people, mostly indigenous peoples, have been displaced by reservoirs worldwide and robbed of their livelihoods from fishing or farming. Serious conflicts are simmering between neighbouring countries because dams have turned off the water supply for downstream states.

The late Indian Prime Minister Jawaharlal Nehru once said: "Dams are India's new temples." Right up to the 1970s, large dams were seen as the synonym for development and economic progress. Dam-building reached its peak between 1970 and 1980, when an average of two to three new large dams per day were commissioned. But a considerable number of the dams analysed by the WCD have fallen short of their technical and economic objectives. Construction cost overruns averaged 56 per cent. Many dams have had negative ecological impacts, and the disadvantages for people living downstream were mostly not taken into account. The planning of dams did not examine sufficiently possible alternatives for meeting power and water needs. There were hardly any retrospective evaluations of dam projects.

### A New Framework for Decision-Making?

Despite this sobering stocktaking, the WCD arrives at an astonishingly simple finding: dams are primarily a means to an end. Their task is to improve the well-being of the people on a sustainable basis. This improvement should be economically acceptable, socially just and environmentally sound. If this goal can be achieved by a dam, its construction should be supported. Where alternative options offer a better solution they should be the preferred choice.

The Commission based its work on a set of five crore values for future decision-making: equity, efficiency, participatory decision-making, sustainability, and accountability. With regard to legal aspects and the extent of the potential risks for those involved, the WCD proposes development of an approach based on recognising rights and assessing risks. All risk-bearers should have a place at the negotiating table.

The WCD also recommends seven strategic priorities for decision-making: gaining public acceptance; comprehensive options assessment; reviewing existing dams; sustaining rivers and livelihoods; recognizing entitlements and sharing benefits; ensuring compliance; and sharing rivers for peace, development and security. These priorities are reinforced by 23 practical criteria and guidelines which can be adopted, adapted and applied by all actors involved in the dam controversy. For instance, the WCD suggests analysing points at issue together with the people affected by existing dams and developing joint proposals for solutions. People affected by new dam projects should be among their favoured beneficiaries, and their claims should be made legally binding.

The report offers a comprehensive compilation of knowledge, which previously was limited to individual case studies or a narrow specialist context, on the social, economic, technological and ecological problems and impacts of large dams. That makes the report a central reference which helps greatly in bringing objectivity into the debate. Provision of an analytical framework and strategic options is certainly an important step. But with regard to its task of developing internationally valid criteria and guidelines for the planning, design, appraisal, building operation, monitoring and shutdown of dams, the report remains very general. What will be decisive here will be to practice with the relevant actors the method and content of the suggested mediation process on the basis of specific cases.

**Deeds Must Follow Words**

The WCD's work must now be made usable for the private sector, civil society and development purpose. What is required is a discussion process involving all major actors. The objective of this process must be the development of practical and effective guidelines in addition to the current standards.

The WCD calls on bilateral development organisations and multilateral development banks to support only dam projects that have resulted from an open process of examining various options. The parties should observe the WCD guidelines. Measures to save water and power should be examined and, if applicable, be promoted.

Private sector companies should publish guidelines on corporate behaviour and acknowledge the WCD principles, criteria and guidelines. Further, the private sector should draw up and implement voluntary codes of conduct, management systems and certification procedures, such as the internationally recognized standard for environmental management (ISO, 14001). The OECD's Anti-Corruption Agreement should be observed, and declarations of honesty incorporated in contracts. Business associations should develop processes to monitor compliance with the WCD guidelines.

NGOs should primarily check compliance with agreements and assist aggrieved parties to seek compensation. They should also assist in identifying relevant stakeholders for dam projects, using the rights and risks approach. Finally the NGOs should build up support networks and partnerships between them.

**Importance of Information**

But do these noble proposals provide the whole answer? the WCD process is based on the opportunities for personal development of every individual in an open society. But it is not enough to build on the negotiating abilities of the potentially affected alone because only specialists can anticipate the complex impacts of dams. Therefore participation presupposes that the mediation process contains a substantial informative component.

Relying solely on a mediation process is also not sufficient in providing for social impacts. There is no generally recognized method to determine the value of 'goods' in a subsistence economy. Without objective criteria, the moral demands on both sides are extremely high. Strategically-motivated behaviour will then not be prevented even if all participants agree readily that the subjective standard of living of people affected by a dam should be improved or at least maintained.

Meditation processes make sense only if agreements are observed. According to the WCD analyses, lack of compliance with agreements is the main cause of the negative social impacts of dams. In the case of dam projects co-financed by international donors, disbursements of funding instalments could depend upon independent evaluations that confirmed compliance. Ensuring compliance is much more difficult in the case of projects financed by the private sector. Because there is no independent institution that could assume the role of arbitrator, it must be in the business world's own interests to act responsibly in ecological and social terms. To be credible, it must provide transparency and independent certifiers.

Due to the opposing interests involved, no-one should expect reaching consensus to be easy. But the example set by the WCD is not the only reason for hope. Taking a closer look at it, the model offers significant advantages for all participants. Partner countries and development organisations wish to continue to use the potential for development which dams will also offer in the future. The private sector will also continue to build and operate dams, and for that they need planning certainly. The advantages for NGOs and the people affected are also obvious.

# Chapter 24

## Water Facts and Findings on Large Dams?

### Water Facts

Today, around 3800 $km^3$ of fresh water is withdrawn annually from the world's lakes, rivers and aquifers. This is twice the volume extracted 50 years ago. World population has passed 6 billion. Projections say that it will reach a peak of between 7.3 billion and 10.7 billion around 2050 before total population begins to stabilise or fall.

50 litres per person per day (or just over 18.25 $m^3$ a year) covers basic human water requirements for drinking, sanitation, bathing and food preparation. In 1990, over a billion people had access to less than 50 litres of water a day. Agriculture accounts for about 67 per cent of withdrawals, industry users 19 per cent and municipal and domestic uses account for 9 per cent.

One-third of the countries in water stressed regions of the world are expected to face severe water shortages this century. By 2025 there will be approximately 6.5 times as many people—a total of 3.5 billion living in water-stressed countries. By the end of the 20th century, there were over 45,000 large dams in over 150 countries. The average large dam today is about 35 years old. Since average construction periods generally range from 5 to 10 years, this indicates a worldwide annual average of some 160 to 320 new large dams per year.

During the 1990s, an estimated $32-46 billion was spent annually on large dams, four-fifths of it in developing countries. Of the $22-31 billion invested in dams each year in developing countries, about four-fifths was financed directly by the public sector. About one-fifth of the world's agricultural land is irrigated, and irrigated agriculture accounts for about 40 per cent of the world's agricultural production.

Half the world's large dams were built exclusively or primarily for irrigation, and an estimated 30 to 40 per cent of the 271 million hectares of irrigated lands worldwide rely on dams. Dams are estimated to contribute to 12-16 per cent of world food production. Hydropower currently provides 19 per cent of the world's total electricity supply, and is used in over 150 countries with 24 of these countries depending on it for 90 per cent of their supply.

Floods affected the lives on average, of 65 million people between 1972 and 1996, more than any other type of disaster, including war, drought and famine. There or 261 water sheets that cross the political boundaries two are more countries. A number of key international rivers lack of basin-wide agreement that defines a process for establishing equitable water use between riparian States.

**Cost Effectiveness**

Cost performance data confirms that large dam projects often incur substantial capital cost overruns. The average overrun was half again as much as the projected cost. The bulk of hydropower projects have delivered power within a close range of pre-project targets but with an overall tendency to fall short of targets.

At current rates, water fees are rarely sufficient to recover both capital and recurrent costs for water supply systems in many developing countries. Growing concern over the cost and effectiveness of large dams and related structural measures as long term responses to floods has led to support for integrated flood management as opposed to flood control.

Multipurpose schemes are inherently more complex and many experience operational conflicts that contribute to under-performance on financial and economic targets. Substantive evaluations of project performance are few in number, narrow in scope, and poorly integrated across impact categories and scales.

**Ecological Costs**

Dams, interbasin transfers, and water withdrawals for irrigation have fragmented 60 per cent of the world's rivers. As a physical barrier the dam disrupts the movement in upstream and downstream species composition and even species loss. In Africa, the changed hydrological regime of rivers has adversely affected floodplain agriculture, fisheries, pasture and forests that constituted the organising element of community livelihood and culture.

Problems may be magnified as more large dams are added to a river system, resulting in an increased and cumulative loss of natural resources, habitat quality, environmental sustainability and ecosystem integrity. Good site selection, such as not building large dams on the main-stem of a river system, and better dam design also played significant roles in avoiding or minimising impacts. The economic appraisal techniques such as risk and distributional analysis were still mandated for only 20 per cent of large dam projects even in the 1990s.

**Social Costs**

At the planning and design stage, an important social impact is the delay between the decision to build a dam and the onset of construction. This can result in communities living for decades starved of development and welfare investments.

The overall global level of physical displacement could range from 40 to 80 million. In India and China together, large dams could have displaced between 26-58 million people between 1950 and 1990. Little or no meaningful participation of affected people in the planning and implementation of dam projects—including resettlement and rehabilitation has taken place.

Empowering people, particularly the economically and socially marginalised by respecting their rights and ensuring that resettlement with development becomes a process governed by negotiated agreements is critical to positive resettlement and rehabilitation.

Poor accounting in economic terms for the social and environmental costs and benefits of large dams implies that the true economic efficiency and profitability of these schemes remains largely unknown.

The direct adverse impacts of dams have fallen disproportionately on rural dwellers, subsistence farmers, indigenous people, ethnic minorities, and women. Where costs and benefits accrue to different groups, the standard procedures for adding up and discounting the expected costs and benefits do not provide an appropriate measure of changes in social welfare.

**Financing**

Almost 2 billion people, both urban and rural poor, have no access to electricity at all. Most efficiency measures and technologies are cost-effective at today's electricity prices and the use of full environmental and social costing of electricity supply options makes them even more so. Among advanced technologies in research and development, micro-turbines and fuel cell show the greatest near and mid-term promise.

Total financing for large dams from multilateral and bilateral development banks comes to more than $4 billion annually at the peak of lending during 1975-84. Although the proportion of investment in dams directly financed by bilaterals and multilateral was perhaps less than 15 per cent. The total investment in dams by the multilaterals and bilaterals since 1950 is approximately $125 billion.

# Chapter 25

## End of Controversy on Large Dams?

Was it worth the effort? The energy, the time, the money invested? Quite a number of people probably put this question to themselves on the 16th of November 2000 when Nelson Mandela launched the final report of the World Commission on Dams (WCD) in London. In an extraordinary process that lasted two and a half years, dam proponents and opponents worked intensely together. Twelve commissioners had tried hard to come up with a consensus on the effects of large dams in the past, and with recommendations for future sustainable planning on water and energy issues. And surprisingly enough: the Commission succeeded. The cost of ten million dollars was financed by governments, international agencies, the private sector, NGOs and various foundations—this is also a novelty. Dam-affected people, non-governmental organisations, companies, consultants, politicians etc. contributed to the processes with their know-how and by giving support and additional resources to the Commission's work.

The establishment of the multi-stakeholder commission was the result of a growing and aggravating controversy about the social, ecological and often enough also economic costs of large dams.

### Global Review Shows Faulty Planning Processes

The WCD Global Review of large dams proves that there were good reasons for massive resistance against large dams in the past. As the report says: "In too many cases an unacceptable price has been paid... especially in social and environmental terms, by people displaced, by communities downstream, by taxpayers and by the natural environment". While funders of large dams, political institutions, consultants and companies claimed in recent years that they had learned from their faults and improved their performance, the WCD highlights that, while policies and assessment procedures have been improved, it appears that business-as-usual too often continued to prevail:

- Even in the 1990s, impacts of downstream livelihoods were not adequately assessed or accounted for in the planning and design of large dams.
- Participation and transparency in planning processes for large dams was neither inclusive nor open, and while actual change in practice remains slow, even in the 1990s, there is increasing recognition of the importance of inclusive processes.
- Where opportunities for the participation of affected people and the undertaking of environmental and social impact assessment have been provided they often occur late in the process, are limited in scope and even in the 1990s their influence in project selection remains marginal.

**Dams Hindered Human Development**

The WCD states that "dams have made an important and significant contribution to human development, and the benefits derived from them have been considerable". A viewpoint that dam-affected people and NGOs hardly share, having in mind the experiences of the past. Medha Patkar, WCD Commissioner and activist in the struggle to save the Narmada river in India wrote in her comment to the Report: "Within the value framework the Commission propagates—equity, sustainability, transparency, accountability, participatory decision-making and efficiency—large dams have not helped attain, but rather hindered 'human development".

The WCD also puts an end to the old viewpoint that the violation of human rights and the social costs that some have to pay can be justified by the benefits for the others. The idea that society as a whole would profit from so-called development that were benefiting from 'trickle down effect'. In fact this development model tends to aggravate social inequities and encourage environmental destruction leaving the rich better of, but the poor more marginalised and resentful. It is not a sustainable model.

**It's Not Just About Dams**

Although it is called the World Commission on Dams the issues before the Commission are much broader. The discussion about large dams is inevitably linked with the need to find solutions for supplying water and energy in the future. To do this in a sustainable way is one of the challenges of our time.

The WCD defined 5 core values that are based on internationally accepted norms like the Universal Declaration of Human Right to Development and the Rio Declaration on Environment and Development:

- Equity
- Efficiency
- Participatory decision-making and Accountability

These values are not really new and some of them have been agreed upon decades ago, but the Global Review of the WCD showed that 'in real life' we are still far from implementing them.

The rights and risks approach of the WCD must be mentioned as an important tool: while funders and dam-builders talk a lot about their (mostly) financial risks, risks of the dam-affected people were not a big issue in the past. The Commission makes an important distinction: while the former take a voluntary risk and have the possibility to decide on whether or not they want to take it, the latter take involuntary risks and so far had hardly any option in deciding on whether or not they are willing to incur them. Rights must not be violated in order to serve the needs of other people. Respecting human rights is the minimum basis for discussion and is not negotiable.

To get better results in the future the WCD defined seven strategic priorities for decision-making:

- Gaining Public Acceptance
- Comprehensive Options Assessment
- Addressing Existing Dams
- Sustaining Rivers and Livelihoods
- Recognising Entitlements and Sharing Benefits
- Ensuring Compliance
- Sharing Rivers for Peace, Development and Security

According to the WCD there are several fundamental strategic points in the decision-making process. One point is right at the beginning of the planning stage: if the discussion about sustainable energy and resources management is carried out in a transparent, open and participatory process, further steps are much more likely to be accepted by all parties and will help prevent conflicts at later project stages. According to the WCD there are several fundamental strategic points in the decision-making process. One point is right at the beginning of the planning stage: if the discussion about sustainable energy and resources management is carried out in a transparent, open and participatory process, further steps are much more likely to be accepted by all parties and will help prevent conflicts at later project stages.

The strategic priority 'Addressing existing dams' includes (among other policy principles) the identification and assessment of outstanding social issues associated with existing large dams. Considering that between 40 and 80 million people have been displaced by large dams (a lot more have been directly or indirectly affected) this is a difficult task. Financial institutions, development agencies and companies are a lot more interested in looking at the future than dealing with the complex problems of the past. But there is no way out. Dam-affected people of the past along with future dam-affected people are unlikely to accept new dams and believe in what is being promised while the legacy of the past is being forgotten. To solve these problems is a condition for further constructive discussions if not a mere moral obligation. How can those responsible for planning future dams think of gaining public acceptance if not by showing that they mean what they say?

The recommendations of the WCD are of fundamental importance, because they were agreed upon in a multi-stakeholder process. In other words, they were made by representative of industry as well as those from dam-affected people, by members coming from industrialized countries as well as those from developing countries. Within the Commission, it was possible to integrate the most diverse views and to come to a consensus.

**No More Dams?**

Although in their assessment the evidence would have allowed even stronger recommendations, NGOs and people's movements welcomed the report and asked for immediate implementation. Other stakeholders do not seem to be very enthusiastic about it. Quite a few representatives from industry and investors seem to fear that the implementation of the WCD recommendations would lead to an abrupt stop in dam building.

All appreciate that the WCD report vindicates many concerns raised by NGO campaigns. Given the role of financial institutions in funding large dams and in the WCD process, and based on the WCD report's recommendations, all has to call on all public financial institutions, including the World Bank, the regional development banks, the export credit agencies and bilateral aid agencies, to take the following actions:

- All public financial institutions should immediately and comprehensively adopt the recommendations of the World Commission on Dams, and should integrate them into their relevant policies, in particular those on water and energy development, environmental impact assessment, resettlement, and public participation. In particular, as recommended by the WCD, no project should proceed without the free, prior and informed consent of indigenous people, and without the demonstrable acceptance of all those who would be affected by the project.
- All public financial institutions should immediately establish independent transparent and participatory reviews of all their planned and ongoing dam projects. While such reviews are taking place, project preparation and construction should be halted. Such reviews should establish whether the respective dams comply, as a minimum with the recommendations of the WCD. If they do not, projects should be modified accordingly or stopped altogether.
- All institutions which share in the responsibility for the unresolved negative impacts of dams should immediately initiate a process to establish and fund mechanisms to provide reparations to affected communities that have suffered social, cultural and economic harm as a result of dam projects.
- All public financial institutions should place a moratorium on funding the planning or construction of new dams until they can demonstrate that they have complied with the above measures.

# Chapter 26

# The Uruguay Round and Agricultural Reform

The Uruguay Round of Multilateral Trade Negotiations (completed in 1994) continued the process of reducing trade barriers achieved in seven previous rounds of negotiations. Among the Uruguay Round's most significant accomplishments were the adoption of new rules governing agricultural trade policy, the establishment of disciplines on the use of Sanitary and Phytosanitary (SPS) measures, and agreement on a new process for settling trade disputes. The Uruguay Round also created the World Trade Organisation (WTO) to replace the General Agreement on Tariffs and Trade (GATT) as an institutional framework for overseeing trade negotiations and adjudicating trade disputes. Agricultural trade concerns that have come to the fore since the Uruguay Round, including the use of genetically engineered products in agricultural trade, state trading, and a large number of potential new members, illustrate the wide range of issues any new round may face.

During the past years since initial implementation of the Uruguay Round agreements, the record with respect to agriculture is mixed. The Uruguay Round's overall impact on agricultural trade can be considered positive in moving toward several key goals, including reducing agricultural export subsidies, establishing new rules for agricultural import policy, and agreeing on disciplines for Sanitary and Phytosanitary trade measures. The Uruguay Round Agreement on Agriculture (URAA) may also have contributed to a shift in domestic support of agriculture away from those practices with the largest potential to affect production and, therefore, to affect trade flows. However, significant reductions in most agricultural tariffs will have to await a future round of negotiations.

**Tariffs, Incentives and Subsidies**

Prior to Uruguay Round, trade in many agricultural products was unaffected by the tariff cuts that were made for industrial products in previous rounds. In the Uruguay Round, participating countries agreed to convert all non-tariff agricultural trade barriers to tariffs (a process called "tariffication") and to reduce them. However, agricultural tariffs remain very high for some products in some countries, limiting the trade benefits to be derived from the new rules. To ensure that historical trade levels were maintained and to create some new trade opportunities where trade had been largely precluded by policies, countries instituted tariff-rate quotas. A tariff-rate quota applies a lower tariff to imports below a certain quantitative limit (quota) and permits a higher tariff on imported goods after the quota has been reached.

The Agreement on Agriculture required countries to reduce outlays on domestic polices that provide direct economic incentives to producers to increase resource use or production. All WTO member countries are meeting their commitments to reduce these outlays, and most countries reduced this type of support by more than the required amount. However, support from those domestic policies considered to have the least effect on production, such as domestic food aid, has increased from 1986-88 levels.

In the Agreement on Agriculture, 25 countries that employed export subsidies agreed to reduce the volume and value of their subsidised exports over a specified implementation period. To date, most of these countries have met their commitments, although some have found ways to circumvent them. The European Union (EU) is by far the largest user of export subsidies, according for 84 per cent of subsidy outlays of the 25 countries in 1995 and 1996. Despite substantial progress in reducing export subsidies, rising world grain supplies and falling world grain prices will make it difficult for some countries to meet future commitments unless they adopt policy changes.

The Uruguay Round's SPS agreement imposed disciplines on the use of measures to protect human, animal, and plant life and health from foreign pests, diseases, and contaminants. The agreement can be credited with increasing the transparency of countries SPS regulations and providing improved means for settling SPS-related trade disputes, including some important cases involving agricultural products. The agreement has also spurred regulatory reforms in some countries. The SPS agreement and the Agreement on Technical Barriers to Trade could provide a framework for disputes over Genetically Modified Organisms (GMOs) brought to the WTO for arbitration.

**Current Issues**

Changes made to the multilateral dispute resolution process in the Uruguay Round may be as important to agricultural trade as the improvement in the substantive rules governing trade in agricultural goods. Initial evidence indicates that the WTO dispute settlement system is a significant improvement over its GATT predecessor. For example, a single country can no longer block the formation of a dispute resolution panel or veto an adverse ruling by blocking the adoption of a panel report. These improvements have led to a number of important agricultural trade cases being adjudicated before the WTO. The outstanding question for the WTO is whether members whose practices have been successfully challenged under the new dispute settlement procedures will live up to their obligations.

Other agriculture-related issues, including a bid for membership by a large and diverse group of potential new

WTO members, the challenge of dealing with State Trading Enterprises (STEs) within WTO disciplines, and issues particular to developing countries, will shape the agenda for future agricultural trade liberalisation discussions. Thirty countries are currently seeking membership in the 134-member WTO. Countries seeking WTO membership accede under conditions negotiated with WTO membership through the privileged trade status with WTO member but may incur adjustment costs in reforming their trade policies and reducing tariffs to meet WTO requirements. Current WTO members gain greater access to the markets of acceding countries.

State trading enterprises, governmental and non-governmental entities that have been granted special rights or privileges through which they can influence trade, continue to be important to the trade of agricultural commodities because many countries consider them to be an appropriate means to meet domestic agricultural policy objectives. Continuing concerns about the trade practices of state trading enterprises in some WTO member countries and the potential accession of China and other countries where STEs are prominent will keep STEs on the WTO agenda.

Developing countries received special treatment in the Uruguay Round, including less stringent disciplines in reforming their trade policies than those apply to developed countries. In the next round of multilateral agricultural trade negotiations, developing countries will continue to have their own interests in the areas of special and differential treatment, export restraints, price stability, food security, food aid, and stock policies. As developing countries identify their positions, coalitions of countries with common trade interests may emerge.

# Chapter 27

## WTO Agricultural Negotiations
### *Completing the Task*

The Cairns Group of 15 agricultural-exporting countries was formed in 1986 to influence agricultural negotiations within the World Trade Organisation (WTO). It was largely as a result of the group's efforts that a framework for reform in farm products trade was established in the Uruguay Round and agriculture was for the first time subject to global trade liberalising rules. The group is positioning itself to play an important role in the new round of WTO agricultural negotiations.

The Cairns Group, which accounts for about 20 per cent of world agricultural exports, includes both developed and developing countries across a diverse set of regions around the world. The group consists of Argentina, Australia, Brazil, Canada, Chile, Colombia, Fiji, Indonesia, Malaysia, New Zealand, Paraguay, Philippines, South Africa, Thailand and Uruguay. By acting collectively, this disparate group has had more influence and impact on the agriculture negotiations than individual members would have had independently. Under Australian leadership, the group takes a consensual approach to decision-making.

**Beyond the Uruguay Round**

Members of the Cairns Group were generally pleased

with the Uruguay Round outcome, but believe much remains to be done to ensure that a genuine market-oriented approach to agricultural policies is achieved. For example, in 1997 levels of agricultural support in Organisation for Economic Cooperation and Development (OECD) countries alone were still extremely high at $280 billion. The approach taken by the group to the challenge of reducing this assistance and creating a freer agricultural marketplace has been in two parts. First, the group has worked to ensure that countries meet the commitments that were agreed to in the agricultural-related agreements during the Uruguay Round. It has done this by remaining visible and active since the end of the round.

Second, the Cairns Group has been effective in engaging other WTO member countries in early preparation for the next round of agricultural negotiations in an attempt to ensure that they start on time and are not unnecessarily protracted as they were during the Uruguay Round. The Cairns Group in April 1998 agreed on a strongly worded "vision statement" conveying the Group's ambition and broad objectives for the 1999 agriculture negotiations and initiated a strategic approach to the preparations for the negotiations. This approach is necessarily ambitious. "The Cairns Group of Agricultural Fair Traders reaffirms its commitment to achieving a fair and market-oriented agricultural trading system as sought by the Agreement on Agriculture. To this end, the Cairns Group is united in its resolve to ensure that the next WTO agriculture negotiations achieve fundamental reform which will put trade in agricultural goods on the same basis as trade in other goods. All trade-distorting subsidies must be eliminated and market access must be substantially improved so that agricultural trade can proceed on the basis of market forces."

**Objectives for Negotiations**

The Vision Statement outlines the Cairns Group's reform goals in three key areas within the Uruguay Round framework, as follows:

- Deep cuts to all tariffs are required, as well as the removal of tariff peaks and the redressing of tariff escalation so that market access for agricultural commodities and value-added agricultural products is on a similar footing as trade in other commercially traded products. This should include the objective of transforming market access barriers to tariffs and removal of non-tariff barriers to trade. In the interim, the Cairns Group supports substantial increases in trade volumes under tariff-rate quotas, while the administration of tariff-rate quotas must not diminish the size and value of market access opportunities, particularly in products of special interest to developing countries;
- All trade-distorting domestic supports must be eliminated or replaced with non-trade distorting methods of assistance. Income aids or other domestic support measures should be targeted, transparent, and fully decoupled so that they do not distort production and trade;
- Export subsidies must be made illegal for agricultural products, as they are for other traded goods, and clear rules must be established to prevent circumvention of export subsidy commitments. In this regard, it is worth nothing that only 25 of the 134 current WTO members are entitled to use export subsidies, and most of these are developed countries (with more than 80 per cent of export subsidies accounted for by the European Union). Also, agricultural export credits must be brought under effective international discipline with a view to ending government subsidisation of such credits.

**Special Needs of Developing Countries**

The vision statement also reaffirms the group's support for the principle of special and differential treatment for developing countries, including least-developed countries and small states, remaining an integral part of the next WTO agriculture negotiations. The Cairns Group ministers agreed that the framework for liberalisation must continue to support the economic development needs, including technical assistance requirements, of these WTO members. As has been stated by the Cairns Group: Major challenges facing many developing countries are the persistence of rural poverty and the linkages between such poverty and serious environmental problems. Consequently, more sustainable agricultural development remains a central policy issue in many developing countries. An improved international trading environment that is more conductive to supporting agricultural development is needed as an essential ingredient in addressing these problems.

Adherence to these principles will not only improve the trading environment for agricultural exporting nations, but will also have important implications for global food security. Food security will be enhanced through more diversified and reliable sources of supply, as more farmers, including poorer farmers in developing countries, are able to respond to market forces and new income-generating opportunities, without the burden of competition from heavily subsidised products. To provide further assurance to net-food-importing countries, export restrictions must not be allowed to disrupt the supply of food to world markets.

Reductions in assistance to the agricultural sector may also have positive implications for the environment. In many cases, agricultural subsidies and access restrictions have stimulated farm practices that are harmful to the environment. Reform of these policies can contribute to the development of environmentally sustainable agriculture.

**Preparations for the Next Round**

Cairns Group ministers welcomed the launch by the second WTO Ministerial Conference in Geneva in May 1998 of preparations for the next round of agriculture negotiations. The WTO Ministerial Declaration that emanated from this conference binds WTO members to a preparatory process that began in September 1998 and will culminate in ministerial agreement on a decision on the scope, structure and time-frame for the agriculture negotiations.

The Cairns Group reaffirms its commitment to achieving a fair and market-oriented agricultural trading system as sought by the Agreement on Agriculture. To this end, the Cairns Group is united in its resolve to ensure that the next WTO agriculture negotiations achieve fundamental reform that will place trade in agricultural goods on the same basis as trade in other goods.

# Chapter 28

## Export Subsidies

### *A Distortion to Free Trade in Agriculture*

Export subsidies are generally considered one of the most distorting trade tools used by governments to interfere with commercial market. Export subsidies allow a government. to determine the level and direction of trade solely on the basis of government subsidies, lowering world prices and denying sales for other, more competitive exporters. Not only are export subsidies unfair commercial tools, but, by encouraging surplus production, they encourage adverse environmental practices, waste government budgets, and may delay restructuring and reform of domestic industries. Substantial progress toward eliminating export subsidies will be a critical element of the World Trade Organisation (WTO) negotiations scheduled to begin at the end of this year.

**The Situation Today**

Under the Uruguay Round Agreement, countries agreed to strictly limit the use of export subsidies. First, products that had not benefited from export subsidies in the past were banned from receiving them in the future. Second, where countries had provided export subsidies in the past, their future use was capped and gradually reduced over 6 to 10 years. Developed countries were required to cut their spending on export subsidies by 36 per cent over six years while also reducing subsidised export quantities by at least 21 per cent on a commodity-specific basis.

Developing countries have until 2005 to cut spending by 24 per cent and subsidised quantities by 14 per cent. Third, countries agreed not to create new schemes that serve as disguised subsidies to get around the product-specific limits. Finally, countries recognised that export credit and food aid programmes were different and exempted them from the new budget and quantity limits, although there was agreement to negotiate disciplines on export credit programmes to ensure that they do not undermine WTO commitments.

Today, the European Union (EU) is the primary export subsidiser—accounting for nearly 85 per cent of the world total. Nearly all other countries agreed in the last round of negotiations not to use or to have only limited recourse to use export subsidies. EU farmers, responding to domestic prices that are often twice the world price, produce more products than can be consumed in Europe, but at such high prices that they can be sold abroad only with generous subsidies. These subsidies force other competitors out of the market and discourage production in countries with comparative advantage.

If the EU's extravagant domestic subsidies are the root cause of export subsidies, they are also putting serious pressure on the whole EU system. The need to impose budgetary discipline on EU farm programmes (annual cost, about $46 billion) is becoming increasingly evident, even in Europe, and the EU's goal of expanding its membership to new countries is putting pressure on it to bring its farm programmes into line with other countries, which will help reduce its need to rely on export subsidies in the future.

### Areas for Resolution

The upcoming negotiations should continue the work begun in the Urguay Round and eliminate existing export subsidies. There is no economic justification for their continued use. By removing subsidised exports, world prices should increase, and farmers, particularly in the EU, will not be artificially encouraged to overproduce products that they cannot grow competitively.

In addition to eliminating export subsidies, countries should examine the rules defining export subsidies to ensure that countries do not resort to other policy tools that might allow governments to distort markets. Specially, WTO members should to look closely at curbing agricultural state trading export monopolies that can exert undue market power or dispose of surplus commodies on a non-market basis. A recent WTO victory by the United States and New Zealand over Canada's special-class system of dairy exports shows that the existing rule against circumvention are effective but must be enforced.

Export credit and food aid programmes were addressed in the Uruguay Round agreement in recognition of the fact that those tools could be disguised as subsidies. These policies may again be on the agenda when the WTO negotiations commence next time. It will be important to ensure that the world's needy continue to have access to imported products, even when financial turmoil rolls would markets and limits the ability of developing countries to meet their food and fiber needs.

Certain large exporting nations—primarily in the EU have used export taxes as a supply management tool by intervening in the market tc restrict exports when domestic stocks are low. These measures can wreak havoc in international markets, exacerbating price swings and reducing the confidence of net-food-importing countries to abandon trade barriers and rely on the international market to provide food security. Similarly, some exporting countries use differential export taxes to discourage exports of basic products (such as grains or oilseeds); they force exporters to process the product domestically (into flour or oil and meal, for example) and export the value added products.

# Chapter 29

## Developing Countries and the WTO Agricultural Negotiations

Developing countries as a group have much to gain from continued progress toward a transparent, rule based trading system in agriculture. The researchers say the negotiations should eliminate export subsidies, impose stricter disciplines on export taxes, cut tariffs, and ensure that food aid continues to be available to poor countries in grant form and delivered so as not to displace domestic production in the countries receiving it. Badly managed food aid, or cheap food imports due to export subsidies, may just reinforce the bias of economic policies against the rural sector. With its negative impact on poor agricultural producers, they say. International research organisations (such as IFPRI, among other institutions) may provide support to developing countries through programmes of collaborative research, technical assistance, and capacity strengthening.

Starting with the first round of trade negotiations under the General Agreement on Tariffs and Trade (GATT) after World War II, there has been a relatively steady trend of increasing multilateral trade liberalisation. The successive rounds of negotiations recognised the greater needs of developing countries, especially since the Tokyo Round. Yet the participation of developing countries was limited. Since many developing countries were not members of GATT, the major forum for airing their views was provided by the United Nations Conference on Trade and Development. The views of developing countries had some impact on the Lome agreements and on aid flows, but had limited influence on negotiations concerning trading rules, which were discussed within the framework of the GATT, where OECD (Organisation for Economic Cooperation and Development) countries set the agenda.

In the Uruguay Round, which began in 1986 and concluded in 1993, developing countries played a larger role in the negotiations compared to previous rounds. In particular, agricultural net exporters organised the Cairns Group (which in addition to Australia, New Zealand, and Canada, included several large developing countries such as Argentina, Brazil, Indonesia, and the Philippines) to pursue their interests. Furthermore, during and after the conclusion of the Uruguay Round, the formal accession of developing countries to the GATT and now the World Trade Organisation (WTO) has continued apace. Of the 134 members of the WTO in February 1999, some 70 per cent were developing countries. The United Nations classified 48 countries as least-developed (LLDCs). Within that group, 29 are members of the WTO, six are in the process of accession, and three are observers. Also, 18 countries have been identified as net-food-importing developing countries (NFIDCs).

**Some Definitions**

The LLDCs are identified by the United Nations General Assembly based on several criteria—income per capita, augmented physical quality of life index, and an index of economic diversification. As a group, they have a population of about 590 million people, with an income per capita about 4 per cent that of the world average (1996). Agricultural production per capita in LLDCs has been declining since the 1970s although the same indicator for all developing countries (mainly under the influence of China) has gone up by nearly 40 per cent in the same period. LLDCs represent a small fraction of world trade (less than 1 per cent for total and about 2 per cent for agricultural trade). They had a positive, although declining net agricultural trade balance until the mid-1980s, when it turned negative. Almost 20 per cent of their total imports are food items.

The 18 net-food-importing developing countries have been selected through a process within the WTO. They have a population of some 380 million people and an income per capita nearly five times that of the LLDC average, but still much lower than the world average. NFIDCs are a diverse group: four are upper-middle income countries; eight are lower-middle income; and six are lower income. Four of them had net food exports on average during 1995-97, but because they imported cereals they are included in the group. NFIDCs' per capita food production as share of both world and developing country averages has risen, although from very low levels.

Although the categories of "developed" and "developing" countries have important legal consequences under WTO rules, there are no formal definitions of either category. The process works through self-identification and negotiation with other member countries of the WTO.

**Completing the Unfinished Agenda**

In general, developing countries operate under what has been called "special and differential treatment". They face lower disciplines and enjoy longer time frames for implementing reforms. In the case of LLDCs, they are totally exempted from WTO commitments, and it has been agreed that developing and least-developed countries should receive special consideration for market access and technical and financial support. Also, during the Uruguay Round, concerns that liberalisation of agricultural policies and trade could adversely affect the food imports of LLDCs and NFIDCs led participants to include several measures dealing with food security issues in the "green box" of permitted domestic support—for instance, the formation of public stockholding and the provision of foodstuffs at subsidised prices. There was a ministerial decision in Marrakesh in April 1994 to deal with possible negative effects of agricultural trade reforms on the food security of LLDCs and NFIDCs. The decision was reemphasised at the 1996 ministerial meeting of the WTO in Singapore.

***Export and Domestic Subsidies:*** While many developing countries have significantly reduced distorting domestic agricultural policies, the possible benefits that these countries and the world can enjoy are thwarted by the subsidies of developed countries. The Uruguay Round was a first step in imposing discipline on the unfair competition arising from subsidised agricultural exports, which hurts poor agricultural producers in developing countries irrespective of their net agricultural trade position. In the next negotiations, that first step should be completed with the elimination of export subsidies. Net-food-importing developing countries should also be interested in stricter disciplines on export taxes and controls that exacerbate price fluctuations in world markets.

Under the Uruguay Round agreement, there is still a lot of scope for the developed countries to use domestic subsidies, in addition to the use of export subsidies; to help their farmers. The developing countries should seek further disciplines in this regard, including, among other things, the elimination of exemptions under the "blue box" (which allows farmers to receive some forms of direct payments that are considered to be trade distorting). Least-developed and developing countries, however, will still be allowed "special and differential treatment" on these issues.

***Market Access:*** If the developing countries are to succeed in diversifying their agricultural sectors, they need expanded access to markets in developed countries. This includes increasing the volume of imports allowed under the current regime of tariff-rate quotas (TRQs, which replaced the previous system of rigid quotas with a combination of a quantitative quota and a high tariff for the eventual out-of-quota imports); making the administration of the TRQs more transparent and equitable; seeking further reductions in tariffs, particularly those still high in some key products; and completing the process of tariffication in the cases where exemptions were granted. Also, eliminating, or at least reducing, tariffs escalation in non-agricultural products is important for developing countries: this practice undermines the possibilities of expanding production and exports of processed goods that use agricultural inputs, exploiting "forward linkages" in the value-added chain.

### What the Most Vulnerable Need

The special situation and concerns of least-developed countries and net-food-importing countries were recognised in a ministerial decision agreed upon at the completion of the Uruguay Round in 1993. These concerns include the preservation of adequate levels of food aid, the provision of technical assistance and financial support to develop the agricultural sector in those countries, and the continuation and expansion of financial facilities to help with structural adjustment and short-term difficulties in financing food imports. It is important to make food aid available in grant form, to target it to poor countries and social groups, and to deliver it in ways that do not displace domestic production in the countries receiving it. Badly managed food aid, or cheap food imports due to export subsidies, may just reinforce the bias of economic policies against the rural sector, with its negative impact on poor agricultural producers.

Volatility in agricultural prices must be monitored carefully. While expansion of world agricultural trade should limit overall fluctuations by spreading supply and demand shocks over larger areas, the decline in world public stocks as a percentage of consumption works in the opposite direction. Improving early warning of potential food shortages, lowering costs for food transportation and storage, and providing better targeted food aid programmes and financial facilities for emergencies are also issues that need to be addressed by countries participating in the coming round of negotiations.

The impact of changes in trade and agricultural policy on poorer consumers and producers in developing countries is a matter of debate. Some have argued that trade liberalisation may hurt both groups. Others have answered that greater productivity and growth coming from better trade and sectoral policies should help generate employment and income, given a setting of adequate overall economic policies and properly functioning markets and social institutions.

Small producers will also be helped by the disciplines that the URAA is bringing to subsidised and dumped exports, while it allows the implementation of a variety of programmes aimed at poor producers or consumers, including stocks for food security purposes and domestic food aid for populations in need. The issue here is the adequate design and funding of domestic policies to achieve the intended objectives of agricultural growth and poverty alleviation, which most certainly will not be helped by trade-distorting interventions either in developed or developing countries.

In general, low-income developing countries and LLDCs should emphasise to the international community the importance of creating and expanding a supportive international trade and financial environment and of implementing an integrated framework for economic and social development, with agricultural and trade polices being an integral part of the strategy. Appropriate measures would include—in addition to the agricultural trade issues suggested here—the continuation and enhancement of the reduction of the external debt of Heavily Indebted Poor Countries (The HIPC initiative) and the further liberalisation of trade in textiles.

But improved international conditions should go hand-in-hand with a better domestic framework in developing and least-developed countries, including stable macro-economic policies, open and effective markets, good governance, the rule of law, a vibrant civil society, and programmes and investments that expand opportunities for all, with special consideration for poor and disadvantaged groups.

**Bringing Developing Countries into the Process**

Developing countries, as small players in the global arena, should be interested and active participants in the design and implementation of international rules that limit the ability of larger countries to resort to unilateral action. Also, domestic legal and institutional frameworks in developing countries may be strengthened by the implementation of internationally negotiated rules that limit the scope for rent seeking and arbitrary projectionist measures. The developing countries as a group have much to gain from continued progress toward a transparent, rule-based, trading system in agriculture.

What are the requirements and skills for the developing countries to become effective members in the next WTO round? Any negotiation requires careful consideration of the legal, economic, and political dimensions that define the substance and possible evolution of the negotiations, as well as the diplomatic and negotiating techniques that may help in the attainment of the expected outcomes. Questions that need to be addressed include:

- What are the economic and social consequences of different WTO scenarios (quantitative estimation of impacts)? Knowing the impacts of alternative scenarios is crucial if developing countries are to represent their interests in the negotiation process;

- What are the legal issues being discussed (definition of obligations, exemptions, time frame, and so on)? Detailed knowledge of international trade law is crucial if developing countries are not to be "short changed." The devil is in the details;

- Looking at the political process, who are the main actors and their interests and what type of alliances may drive the negotiations? Negotiators must understand the political economy of their own country and of other countries in the WTO if they are to negotiate effectively;

- With these elements, an adequate diplomatic and negotiating strategy must be defined and implemented.

Developing countries that have carefully considered all four components will be better prepared to participate effectively in the coming negotiations. Of course, limited financial and human resources act as an important constraint. However, developing countries may overcome some of the problems through collective action, for instance considering the creation of alliances with respect to their main export and import commodities and the markets they approach for their exports. An example is the Cairns Group. This approach could reduce the fixed costs of negotiations. Spreading them over groups of countries, allow a better use of scarce technical expertise, and improve the bargaining position of developing countries. It could also be in the interest of the OECD countries to deal with negotiating blocs, which represent a smaller number of negotiating positions, rather than with numerous separate countries. The negotiations would be much more efficient and balanced.

# Chapter 30

## The Future of Agricultural Trade

In the Uruguay Round, countries recognised that the long term solution for agriculture did not lie in administered prices, trade restrictions, supply controls and export subsidies but rather in open, non-distorted markets. It is the time to take bold steps toward bringing agricultural trade into the 21st century by accelerating agricultural trade reform.

There are four key areas for accelerating reforms: eliminating export subsidies; increasing market access through substantial tariff cuts and expansion of tariff rate quotas; cutting further trade-distorting domestic subsidies; and ensuring technical standards are based on sound science.

The world's farmers and ranchers are facing two difficult challenges at the dawn of the 21st century. First, they are being asked to provide more products at lower cost, higher quality, greater variety, and in a safer manner than ever demanded before. Second, they are being asked to produce this abundance on a shrinking natural resources base that is often subject to government regulations. Meeting these global challenges will require unleashing the production potential of world agriculture while practising proper environmental stewardship. The ingenuity and hardwork we usually associate with farmers will be essential to meet these challenges, but they will not be sufficient unless we further reform agricultural trade to create an environment that rewards risk and investment and encourages efficiencies.

**Today's Agricultural Challenges**

Farmers are responsible for feeding a rapidly growing world population. And despite progress over the years, too many people still are not getting enough food. Many countries including the United States, are working vigorously to promote technological innovations to meet the need for food and fiber in the coming years. However, as important as this work is, it is only part of the solution. These technologies and the hard work of the world's farmers need a trading environment that encourages investment and efficient production, and generates economic growth to finance production and consumption needs long-term trends in agriculture pose serious challenges for all farmers. The same technological advances that increase yields may result in lower prices. Increasing social concerns about effect of agricultural production on the environment and living conditions result in new restrictions on farm activities. As urban dwellers and industry stake competing claims for land, water and energy, many producers find their ability to farm made ever more difficult.

Two approaches to organising the agricultural economy present a stark contrast in dealing with these challenges. One model, popular in Europe and Asia, is to retain an inward-looking agricultural system focused on supply control and government regulation geared to keeping farm prices high and, since guaranteed high prices are a drain on the treasury, to controlling production. Under this approach, bureaucrats try to assess the optimal level of national production—not so little that imports are needed and not so much that excess production; must be bought at high prices and then dumped on world markets. This "command-and-control" structure stifles farmer efficiency and ingenuity and distorts world markets, especially as subsidised surpluses are regularly exported; and it does not address the challenge to farmers to produce food for the next century. It also ignores the interest of domestic consumers (who have to pay high internal prices) and producers in other countries (who have to compete with subsidised products). Of biggest concern is that the anti-market policies of this approach hamstring the agriculture sector from pursuing the technological advances needed to meet its future challenges.

Another approach is to place agriculture on a more market-oriented basis, particularly by removing trade barriers and reducing trade-distorting policies. Greater market orientation was the principle that actions agreed to in the last set of multilateral trade negotiations. In the Uruguay Round, countries recognised that the long-term solution for agriculture did not lie in administered prices, trade restrictions, supply controls, and export subsidies but rather in open, non-distorted markets. Now is the time to take bold steps toward bringing agricultural trade into the 21st century by accelerating agricultural trade reform.

**The Gains from Trade**

The benefit from free and fair trading of agricultural products have immediate effects on people. Eliminating trade barriers and reducing unfair competition will help ensure that farmers have incentives to produce and consumers have access to the products they desire. Liberalising agricultural trade will contribute to better resource allocation by farmers, which has conservation benefits, rewards low-cost producers, encourages efficiencies, and removes the drag on economic growth.

Opening trading opportunities also increases the food security of food-importing countries by giving supplier countries the confidence required to put more land into production and to create marketing relationships. Trade provides consumers with year-round access to a greater variety of less expensive products, while rewarding producers who are able to find and meet specific consumer demands for high-value products. In a broader context, by allowing imports that are more efficiently produced elsewhere, trade encourages specialisation in efficient agricultural and non-agricultural production.

More dramatically, trade literally saves lives. Without the international flow of food products from areas with abundant production to areas where food is scarce, many people in the world would be eating less or not at all. Trade has dynamic effects, as well, that push long-term productivity growth. For example, access to customers in overseas markets creates an incentive for technological innovation, resulting in exciting developments in improved seed varieties and production techniques. International markets also expand market outlets, raising prices and giving producers increased confidence to produce more than required merely for national needs, allowing productive farmers to not only feed their neighbours but literally feed the world.

Equally important, trade in agricultural products is becoming increasingly critical to farm and ranch incomes. Increased productivity and often times flat domestic demand increases the importance of reliable international markets. Foreign markets are not just a dumping ground for surplus products; overseas consumers value choice and quality, particularly when producers in their own country cannot meet their demands or when they are charged inflated prices. Consequently foreign and value-added agricultural producers, raising farm-gate prices and helping support the range of agriculture-related industries.

Political reality also encourages a focus on international markets; policies based on high government guaranteed prices are ultimately politically untenable because they are hugely expensive, unresponsive to the needs of customers and producers, insensitive to environmental and agronomic realities, and a shameful waste of economic assets. Rather than farming government programmes, our producers are looking for customers around the world.

While agricultural trade benefits consumers and producers alike, it is an area in which progressive reform is ardently opposed by entrenched domestic interests. Producers in some countries, cosseted by high guaranteed prices and protective tariffs, oppose any move toward greater market orientation. Intervention in the agricultural economy—measured by the Organisation for Economic Cooperation and Development by summing price supports, direct payments, and other support as a per cent of total agricultural production—has actually increased in some countries from the levels at the beginning of the Uruguay Round. In the last set of multilateral trade negotiations, countries began the process of dismantling protection and delinking farm support from production decisions. Consequently, reforms have been undertaken by some countries.

### The WTO Opportunity

The major objective in the upcoming farm talks is to accelerate the reform process initiated in the Uruguay Round. That means further substantial negotiations on tariffs, subsidies, and other trade-distorting measures so that the level and other trade-distorting measures so that the level and direction of trade are determined by market forces, not government intervention. Four key areas are outlined below:

*(i)* ***Export Competition:*** Export subsidies are the most distorting trade tool because the level and direction of trade is directly determined by government subsidies. Today, the European Union (EU) is the only substantial export subsidizer—nearly all other countries agreed not to use, or have only limited resource to use, export subsidies in the last round of negotiations. EU farmers, responding to domestic prices frequently twice the world price, produce more products than can be consumed in Europe, but at such high prices that they can be sold abroad only with generous subsidies. These subsidies push other competitive supplies out of the market (which is expensive and unfair) and discourage production in countries that have a comparative advantage in agricultural production (which is wasteful and is threatening both to the environment and to future farm production needs).

**In the Uruguay Round negotiations, countries acknowledged the corrosive nature of subsidies and agreed to cap and reduce their use. The upcoming negotiations should eliminate them to ensure that countries do not resort to other policy tools that allow government spending to determine winners in the marketplace. Specifically, WTO members should look closely at curbing distorting state trading agricultural export monopolies that can disguise subsidies and exert distorting market power, along with other policies used to dispose of surplus commodities on a non-market basis.**

*(ii)* ***Market Access:*** Measure applied at the border to stop trade currently are the principal barrier to a freer and more open trading environment for agriculture. Market access barriers deny efficient producers the chance to compete in other market and limit the variety and quality of products available to consumers. Opening markets and maximising trade opportunities are fundamental principles of WTO, and we still have a long way to go in agriculture to open markets to competition.

The Uruguay Round Agreement set agricultural trade on a more predictable basis by requiring that all non-tariff measures, such as quotas and import bans be converted to simple tariffs. While this was a necessary first step to removing trade barriers, many of the tariffs are still prohibitively high. For example, while the average tariff assessed by the United States on agricultural products is less than 5 per cent (and nearly zero for industrial products), the average agriculture tariff-ratequota (TRQ). Where only specific quantities of imports receive low duties. Many other commodities also; are subject to high tariffs.

As we start the next century, higher tariffs should not stop the flow of imported agricultural products. Where TRQs remain as a transitional step before we achieve more open trade, we expect more specific disciplines on the way in which they are administered. Similarly, we need to take a hard look at agricultural state trading monopoly. Importers; use of these state traders may have been justifiable when more restrictions allowed on farm trade, but in the tariff—only regime it is hard to see why a government needs to insert itself between an exports and an end-user.

***(iii)Domestic Subsidies:*** Domestic subsidy programmes are often the root cause of other distorting polices. Subsidy policies that increase domestic prices above world price levels can be maintained only if price-competitive imports are restricted. Additionally, overproduction generated by high domestic prices can be sold on world markets only with export subsidies that bring the price down to the world price. While reining in distortive domestic subsidy programmes has value in its own right for rationalising agricultural production, the WTO negotiations will focus on their trade-distorting elements.

In the Uruguay Round negotiations, countries agreed to distinguish trade-distorting subsidies (generally those linked to the production of a specific crop or related to price supports) from non-trade distorting subsidies (such as research and development, training and environmental production). The trade-distorting subsidies were capped, and the process of reducing allowable levels of subsidies began. This distinction is a good one: the nasty sort of subsidy that distorts markets and straitjackets producers should be cut, while programmes that will increase a country's ability to produce agricultural products in the next century without distorting production incentives should not be reduced.

***(iv) Standards:*** As WTO members make progress on cutting tariffs and subsidies, the temptation increase to disguise trade barriers as health and safety measures or other innocuous-sounding "technical standards". Moreover, when regulations purportedly designed to protect heath are instead vehicles for domestic protectionism, the credibility

> of the entire safety apparatus of a country is put up for questioning. When good science is replaced by politics, the basis for sound health policy is undermined. Therefore, increasing government accountability by putting the emphasis on sound science for health standards should discipline disguised barriers to trade and strengthen health policy.

In the Uruguay Round, countries agreed to a set of sound principles: each has the right to maintain health and safety measures, but these must be based on sound science, backed by scientific evidence and an assessment of the risk, and be no more trade-restrictive than required to meet health goals. In practice, countries have found that these principles work well—bogus measures adopted without scientific basis have been successfully challenged in the WTO without sacrificing health concerns. Creating a supportive environment for the propagation of yield-enhancing biotech products also is critical for meeting the needs of the coming century.

**Agriculture is Different**

Agriculture occupies a special place in the national economies of most countries around the world. Farmers are responsible for feeding and clothing people. Farming also holds a powerful claim on our national cultures that calls for the preservation of rural lifestyles and values. Farm production is subject to the cruel vagaries of weather and the relentless decline in prices and increases in costs. Some people point to these factors as justifying a different treatment for agriculture in the international economy, including justifying trade-distorting agricultural policies. This is wrong-headed; societies can support farms and preserve rural communities in ways that foster choice, protect natural resources, and expand trade.

Farm production in the next century cannot afford to be trapped in a static system in which prices are determined by government mandate, production decisions are controlled by central planners, and farmers are forced to produce only for local consumers. This myopic system cannot be sustained in any important agriculture producing society. Moreover, this type of system will not meet the needs of the coming century, when we will face unprecedented consumer demand and natural resource constraints.

Instead, I look forward to dynamic world of agricultural trade in which producers, exporters and retailers apply the creativity of the human mind to the natural bounty of the earth. In this "new" world, we will produce a greater amount and variety of food than ever before, feed the coming billions, sustain our environment, and unlock economic resources otherwise stifled by moribund protectionism, ultimately raising living standards around the world.

# Chapter 31

## Opening Markets for Agriculture

While the Uruguay Round made a good start—more was done to liberalise agricultural trade and to being agriculture into the system than in all previous rounds combined—we have to recognise that agriculture still has a long way to go to complete its reform and to be fully integrated into the world trading system. Prior to the Uruguay Round, agricultural trading rules were not in concert with other sectors. The Uruguay Round Agreement (URAA) made good first steps towards bringing agriculture into conformity with international trade rules governing other goods, but much remains to be done.

The Uruguay Round, of course, required certain reductions in trade-distorting measures, and the implementation of those reforms has proceeded very well. Two other legacies of the Uruguay Round are very important for the new negotiations—a mandate to continue what was begun, and a structure for achieving liberalisation. The WTO's "built-in" agenda includes agriculture. It was recognised from the outset that the first period of reform that we are still implementing was only a down payment.

In addition to the commitment to continue negotiations, the URAA—focusing on export subsidies, market access and domestic support—established a structure on which to build. Establishing a three-pillar structure was the most time-consuming undertaking in the round. Fortunately, we do not need to reinvent that wheel. The structure of the rules provides a logical approach for the negotiations, one which most seem to agree we should keep and build on.

**Export Competition**

Export subsidies are an illegitimate policy instrument, a symptom of a systemic imbalance in a nation's agricultural policies, the costs of which are borne by others. The costs of domestic policy choices should be borne by the country that chooses them, not foisted onto its trading partners by subsidising exports. The Uruguay Round made a start at eliminating agricultural export subsidies: 36 per cent reduction of budget expenditures on export subsidies and 21 per cent reduction of quantities over a six-year implementation period. With experience to show that markets adapt, we should now be able to improve the pace of export subsidy reductions and eliminate the export subsidy scourge from agricultural trade. Export subsidies are not allowed in the WTO rules for any other industry. Their use constitutes a source of trade distortion and degradation to the environment, and there is no valid reason to keep them any longer.

**Market Access**

The Uruguay Round progress on market access leaves much to be done. It left tariffs too high and it did not create much new market access. The average non-agricultural tariff is now 4 per cent, while the average agricultural tariff is over 40 per cent, and tariffs on some products exceed 300 per cent. With a few exceptions, non-tariff barriers were converted to tariffs, and members were required to open up at least a small minimum access—3 per cent of domestic consumption initially, growing to 5 per cent by the end of the adjustment period—under tariff-rate quotas.

The stage has been set for real reforms. Let access continue to grow and let all tariffs be reduced to a negotiated maximum level by the end of the transition period. In addition, an examination of the administration of tariff-rate quotas should lead to transparent and open systems.

Many WTO members note that importers were required to change non-tariff barriers to tariffs and grant access, while no reciprocal disciplines were imposed on export restraints of exporting countries. Net food importing countries should be able to expect that if they open their border to international market, those international markets will deliver supplies as reliably to importers as to the domestic markets of exporters. Willingness on the part of leading exporting members to discipline export controls will reassure "food security" countries that expanding market access is not risky.

**Domestic Support**

The Aggregate Measure of Support was a success as a component of the Agreement on Agriculture and the insistence on reducing trade-distorting measures. The drive toward decoupled support ("green box") is the key. By the end of 1996, the United States had largely decoupled farm programmes so that payments to farmers were not linked to a requirement to produce. Other WTO members will also succeed in orienting their policies toward market signals. In the new round, further review and decreases in the aggregate measure of support will clearly lead to market-based agricultural trade.

A new buzzword that some countries are using to justify domestic support is "multi-functionality" It is a buzzword for what everybody in agriculture has known for thousands of years: agriculture serves other purposes besides producing food and fibre. But the real problem with the discussion of multi-functionality is not semantic. It is the confusion between policy goals and policy instruments. If the United States appears skeptical about the implications of multi-functionality for WTO rules, the US objection is not multi-functionality as a factual matter. Each country chooses social objectives for themselves. There is no inherent connection between those objectives and trade-distorting agricultural policies.

**New Issues**

While the Uruguay Round established effective disciplines in traditional problem areas, such disciplines have not yet been established in some new areas. As monopolies, state trading enterprises (STEs) can distort trade and they frequently operate behind a veil of secrecy. The agricultural trading system has much to gain from WTO disciplines on STEs because they allow some countries to undercut exports based on open market transactions and restrict imports.

Biotechnology holds tremendous promise globally for food consumers, producers, and the environment. With the world's population growing by about 2 per cent annually, there are 80 million more mouths to feed each year. Some countries threaten to adopt policies regarding the importation and planting of bio-engineered crops and the labelling of products containing bio-engineered foods that are not based on scientifically justified principles. If our farmers are to meet the challenge of feeding an ever-increasing population with a sustainable agricultural system, then they must have access to the new bio-engineeed varieties. We need to think about how the WTO can help facilitate this new technology.

**Developing Countries**

One of the critical components to a successful new round of negotiations will be the full participation of a substantially increased number of developing countries. Open trade in agriculture relieves farmers in developing countries of the burden imposed by protectionism and export subsidies, while reducing hunger and offering reliable supplies of food at reasonable prices.

# Chapter 32

## Rural Poverty in India and Development as a Policy Challenge

Poverty can be overcome, and that the poor can increase their income and production within an appropriate framework. Part of that framework is made up of a flow of resources and local-level institutional development, and there is considerable scope for improvement in both. However, the impact of investment and organisation is strictly determined by the nature of the policy environment. While project and programmes can bring some relief to the rural poor, substantial change needs a strong policy commitment. While the poor can overcome poverty, they will not be able to until this becomes a major focus of national policy and action. In the main, this sort of commitment has not been made in the past—at the expense of both the poor and overall development in many areas.

The current state of India is highly contradictory. On the one hand, there is proclamation of a new order; on the other, increasing value is given to sectional and short-term national and group interests. With an overt concern with the India's poor goes an equal weight given to concern with economic mechanisms and relations that pay little attention to poverty and foster more inequality. The dangers of this situation are real. The lack of concrete attention being given to change will mean greater economic polarisation. Greater polarisation among the better-off, and between the better-off and the poor—means instability and a lack of consensus, a lack of legitimacy.

Poverty is far-reaching, and ought to be curtailed. In a period in which resources everywhere appear restricted, this seems not to be an attractive proposition at the practical level. Welfare is everywhere giving way to production as an imperative, just as public expenditure is giving way to private accumulation. Poverty alleviation does not appear to be an idea whose time has come. The objections are great, but they are also misplaced. Poverty alleviation is not necessarily a drain upon accumulation, and it is not primarily a public activity. Poverty alleviation is primarily the activity of the poor themselves, and their progress necessarily involves productive expansion. If this potential for private expansion has not been realised, it is not because of the nature of the poor, it is because of the way in which national economic affairs have been organised. Economic policy has been oriented towards the better off—not infrequently at the expense of the poor. Given the historic association between wealth and power, the definition of development in terms of the large and the wealthy is hardly surprising.

There is the possibility of associated growth involving both large-scale and small-scale production, the better of and the poor. The realisation of this possibility might result from a new social compact. This social compact is not a commitment to social safety nets and welfare, both of which seem to presuppose that the poor are somehow necessarily out of the growth field. It is a commitment to abolishing artificial and onerous terms of exchange that discriminate against the poor, to investing resources where there are real opportunities for gain, irrespective of whether the economic agents concerned are rich or poor, and to creating the space for the poor to organise to pursue their social and economic interests.

There is a need for a new growth model consistent with new social realities. While the 1980s was a period of clearing away many of the obstacles to development, it was not a period in which there emerged a clear vision of what represented the positive basis for growth, beyond, that is, a general prescription of market-driven operations. The model must pass from admonition to positive prescription to fuel growth by integrating the poor in their rightful place in the production function. It must redefine the position of public expenditure in the development process, and seek to establish market structures which are both equitable and open to the participation of the economically weaker elements of the population. Most of all it must revalue the position and contribution of the poor and small-scale producers in the growth process, particularly in the agricultural sector, but not exclusively agriculture.

This means that the issue is not so much one of less government, but of government, both national and local, finding a new rationale for action, including, *inter alia*, creating conditions that will effectively unleash the productive potential of the rural poor.

Financial flows to the poorest Indians are not likely to undergo a very major expansion, especially through private channels. Development will rely very much on the mobilisation of their own resources, and many of these resources are in the hands of the poor, are, indeed, not only the human capital embodied in the poor but also their assets which, while small, individually are cumulatively important in India. The growth model for the 1990s will have to embrace that fact, and build upon it. The paradox of most development models is that they have emphasised the value of what Indians do not have, while devaluing what they have: capital intensity has been promoted in situations of scarcity of capital, at the expense of abundant labour and of low-cost methods of manifold increase of the productivity of assets of which the poor do dispose. In a not very indiret way, the creation of poverty has been subsidised. Poverty alleviation is neither a special topic nor a low-cost substitute for growth. Is is neither more nor less "social" than development in general. It is part of the formulation of any sustainable strategy of economic development. In the 1990s it may, and perhaps should, become the dominant issue—not as an alternative to the structural reorganisations of the 1980s, but as a means of filling a growth framework with substance.

# Chapter 33

## Crisis Prevention

### *Can Better Development Planning Lessen the Toll of Civil Emergencies and Natural Disasters?*

Even a cursory scan of the world's headlines is depressing: armed conflicts are grinding on in Somalia, Afghanistan and in a growing number of other countries. And the effects of natural disasters are becoming more catastrophic each year. International relief aid, in response to such emergencies, has increased substantially. But how large can these sums of money realistically be expected to grow? With no end in sight to the need for relief, the good will of international donors is quickly giving way to disillusionment.

This leads us to a second question, which is, where does development fit in this grim scenario? For the development community to remain aloof from the issue of disasters and emergencies is not only politically short sighted, it also ignores totally the causes and the effects of such phenomena.

Natural hazards such as hurricanes and earthquakes may be impossible to prevent. But they only become natural disasters if people are vulnerable. Why is it, for example, that an earthquake in Khilari, Maharashtra that registered 6.9 on the Richter scale killed up to 35,000 people, when an earthquake of almost the exact same magnitude in Los Angeles in 1994 claimed only 57 lives? By reducing poverty we can help increase the coping capacity of vulnerable populations. Therefore helping people lower such vulnerability is as much a development issue as the environment, or women's participation in development. Moreover, the repercussions of natural disasters go far beyond the immediate casualty list that so transfixes the media. Secondary and longer-term effects can be equally if not more devastating. And they must be taken into account by developing practitioners.

It has been estimated, for example, that the damage to Mexico City's infrastructure form a massive 1985 earthquake amounted to US $3.6 billion. Yet over the subsequent five years, the negative ripple effect on that country's balance of payments resulted in a loss of $8.6 billion. Furthermore, reconstruction requirements forced Mexican authorities to revise their economic policies to meet an increased demand for public funding, credits and imports. The priorities for public expenditure were redirected to reconstruction projects, leaving many of the pre-disaster problems of the city and its people unattended.

In Bangladesh, floods in the recent past 2,000 people. But on closer examination we find that the toll was much more expensive than that: in each of these years the country's economic growth rate was halved by the delayed planting of rice and the destruction of seedbeds in the floods, further undermining the country's food security. All of these are consideration that go beyond relief, but they must be taken into account by development professionals.

Other emergencies may be more complex, but must be subjected to the same analysis. As the situations in Angola, Burundi, Somalia and the former Yugoslavia demonstrate, we know little about the dynamics of emergencies that arise from civil conflict. We do know, however, that their cause usually lies in a lethal mix of poverty, poor governance and ethnic or religious rivalries exacerbated by profound social inequities. We are also learning that their resolution frequently requires the application of peacekeeping and political measures, combined with relief and development. Among the most virulent effects of such complex emergencies is the massive displacement of people; women and children are the principal victims, constituting 70 per cent of the world's refugees.

These complex emergencies around the world could easily get worse before they get better. This being said, carefully designed development efforts—carried out as building blocks to national reconciliation in the fragile post-conflict stage will need to increase commensurately. The appropriateness and the sustainability of these development efforts will be one of the most important factors in determining whether peace itself becomes sustainable. For example, the absence of carefully tailored reintegration strategies for demobilised soldiers and their host communities would be an almost open invitation to resumed violence.

Yet we must also be conscious of the impact of aid and try harder to prevent the need for relief in the first place. An increasing body of evidence suggests for example that emergency aid can sometimes be counter-productive in the longer-term, increasing the vulnerability of populations and impeding recovery. Ironically, we find ourselves in situation today where it is far easier to obtain funds for maintaining refugees in their places of asylum than for helping them reintegrate into their own societies. In such cases, we may very well be helping to perpetuate the problem that we sought to relieve, as the presence of large numbers of refugees is sometimes itself a cause of conflict.

So how are we to proceed? And what exactly is the nature of the relief to development continuum that remains logical in the abstract but elusive in reality? The concept of a continuum does not imply a linear and absolutely progressive set of responses. On the contrary, it means that we are dealing with a set of processes rather than rigidly defined steps. It also means that development must be very much part of the disaster management process, and that the aim of the continuum must be to move from relief to rehabilitation and resumed development at the earliest opportunity. However, this resumed development must include conscious measures to reduce the vulnerability that caused the disaster or the emergency in the first place.

In other words, we must give greater thought to prevention before we reach for the "cure"—for humanitarian, political and financial reasons. (The Japanese insurance industry spends $200 million a year on disaster education alone). And as development practitioners, we must reconcile ourselves to the vastly more complicated environment in which we have to operate.

This means, for example that we will have to begin examining whether the economic policy "medicine" often prescribed will reduce conflict or enhance it. We will have to ask ourselves if the reconstruction period following a civil conflict or natural disaster is the right time to advocate cuts in social spending, as has happened in certain countries in Africa and Latin America. Similarly, is it really in children's best interests to build a school in a seismic zone without first ensuring its structural stability? And does it really make sense to urge drought-prone countries to increase their reliance on cash crops, as has been done in some instances.

A story that never made headlines anywhere involves hundreds of the poorest people in Bangladesh, whose homes remained intact during the floods of 1988, when many others were simply washed away. These people were fortunate enough to have obtained credit through the Grameen Bank for construction materials as well as instruction in the building of flood-resistant homes. The Grameen revolving fund had received start-up capital from International Financial Agencies. Since that time the effort has been expanded, and more than 10,500 flood-resistant homes have been built in the last two years.

This is just one example of the kind of action we need more of—in fairly predictable and recurring circumstances such as the floods in Bangladesh, as well as in the more complex, man-made emergencies to which we must respond.

# Chapter 34

## Finance Matters

### *Financial Liberalisation Too Much Too Soon?*

An efficient and stable financial system is important for economic growth and poverty reduction. The financial crises that have afflicted many countries in recent times have been a costly and painful reminder of the disastrous consequences for development of weak financial markets. The recurrence of financial crises, at both the international and national levels, and the adverse effect they have had on economic growth and poverty levels, have highlighted the need for a policy framework which addresses the inherent vulnerability of financial markets to systemic instability and failure.

Governments have always intervened in the financial sector and there are sound theoretical and practical reasons for doing so. Financial markets are characterised by problems of limited and unequal information, making them inherently imperfect and prone to failure. Financial regulation and supervision are therefore essential for efficient and stable financial market development. How should governments intervene? Have financial liberalisation and financial sector reform made financial systems more, or less vulnerable to instability and systemic crises? How can the process be better managed? What is the best policy framework for supporting financial sector development in low-income countries.

**Repression to Liberalisation**

For many years, governments followed a policy of financial 'repression', which relied on fixing interest rates below market levels and controlling the allocation of credit. The economic distortions induced by these policies were considerable. Financial systems remained under developed, lending patterns were inefficient and failed to achieve their distributional goals. Negative real interest rates led to low savings and encouraged capital flight. Macro-economic performance also deteriorated countries with large negative real interest rates experienced lower location efficiency and growth rates. In the state owned banking sector, poor lending decisions (often politically influenced) and low repayment rates led to bank insolvency and large budgetary bailouts of depositors and creditors.

A growing awareness of the economic costs of financial 'repression', led to financial 'liberalisation' as the dominant policy paradigm over the past two decades. Initially, the relaxation of controls on interest rates was the focus for financial reform which was often triggered by a financial crisis. The relaxation of controls on the financial sector was often part of a more general policy shift towards liberalisation of the domestic economy and opening out the international economy liberalisation soon broadened therefore beyond interest rate liberalisation, to include a wide range of measures constituting a programme of financial sector reform was adopted under World Bank sectoral or structural adjustment lending conditionalities, the key elements of which included privatisation of banks, entry of new domestic and foreign entrants into the banking sector, bank restructuring and recapitalisation, opening upto the capital account, strengthening bank regulation and supervision institutions.

**Has Financial Liberalisation Worked**

The period of financial liberalisation conincided with, or was soon followed by heightened financial instability, culminating in the dramatic financial crisis in East Asia in the second-half of the 1990s. Clearly, financial liberalisation has not led to a smooth transition to a stable and efficient financial system. It would be wrong, however, to jump to the easy, but shallow, conclusion that financial liberalisation has 'failed'. Firstly, the fact that the period of increased systemic instability does not prove causality. Secondly, no process of change comes cheap: a reasoned assessment of the costs and benefits of the policy changes is needed. And thirdly, what would have been the outcome without the policy change. Finally, the impact of financial liberalisation will differ between countries, depending on each country's economic and institutional characteristics. The more relevant research issue, therefore, relates to the design and timing of context-specific policy measures, which will contribute to the development of an efficient and stable financial system. Could financial liberalisation have been managed better? If so, what policies are now needed? The commercial banks are the dominant component of the financial sector in low-income countries and are critical to the efficiency and stability of the financial system as a whole. Financial liberalisation was associated with a shift in prudential regulation from direct regulation of banks, by for example, regular site visits, to an indirect approach based on the monitoring of bank capital to ensure that it remained adequate in relation to the risk being taken. Additional regulatory measures are also necessary to restrain the activities of the privitised and other newly-established private banks. The regulatory and supervisory framework may also need to be extended, to cover micro-finance institutions which have developed significant deposit taking capacity.

Four main obstacles to efficient banking regulations are:

*(a)* Information, contracting and monitoring problems;

*(b)* Lack of supervisory personnel;

*(c)* High operational costs; and

*(d)* Poor credibility and regulation of regulatory bodies. The appropriateness of various policy measures for

dealing with these constraints are discussed and ranked in terms of their suitability for low-income countries. What are the implications of allowing micro-finance institutions to offer a range of financing services beyond small-scale lending.

**Too Much, Too Soon?**

The experience with financial liberalisation reveals a strong correlation between liberalisation and financial crisis. This can be explained partly by the exposure of existing inefficiencies and distortions in the financial structure, and partly by a failure to develop a strong regulatory and supervisory framework, prior to liberalisation. Weakness in the initial conditions affect the ability of the privatised banks and new market entrants, to operate on broadly commercial principles. Borrowers are often unable to service their loans, due to poor quality lending and high interest rates. Liberalisation of the capital account increases the inflow of foreign capital, but at the same time threatens that stability of the financial institutions by increasing the exchange rate and domestic lending risks.

The existing regulatory and supervisory system may be unsuited to a market-based environment. Consequently, across-the-broad 'big-bang' financial liberalisation and financial sector reform increase the likelihood of systemic crisis, where the institutional and human resource environment is weak. Much of the blame for post-liberalisation financial crisis lies, therefore, with the scale and sequencing of financial reform. What is needed is a more gradual and considered approach to financial liberalisation, which recognises that institutional strengthening, especially in the regulation and supervision capacity, is a prerequisite and supervision capacity is a prerequisite for creating a more efficient and stable financial sector which can contribute fully to achieving economic growth and poverty reduction in developing countries.

# Chapter 35

## Economics and Environment

Statistics change our view of the world. So statistics, however objective and accurate, are never value free but focus on what societies deem important. For better or worse, they guide government, business and individual decisions.

Until recently, the old game of India's economic growth was unquestioned and the score was kept between the national players by comparing their Gross National Product (GNP) or its narrower domestic version, Gross Domestic Product (GDP). It is time to take a closer look at the proliferation of new scoreboards, statistics and quality-of-life indexes which will redefine wealth and progress and change the future direction of human society.

### Clarifying Values

These new scorecards and the 'greening' of GNP/GDP national accounts reflect the new 'green' accounting in thousands of balance sheets, reports and books on environment. At the very least, assumptions underlying old and new indicators are being clarified. The debate is still over what rather than how to measure, and what to do about values and amenities that are priceless.

The costs of GNP growth are now obvious—from felled forests, pollution exhausted soils, depleted natural resources and holes in the ozone layer to disrupted cultures and communities.

The concept of GNP/GDP was adapted into national accounting in India. With little re-examination, it continues to value bombs and bullets (defence expenditure), highly while setting the values of defence expenditure, education and public infrastructure—not to mention clean air and water and other environmental assets—at zero. It also ignores the some 50 per cent of production, which is unpaid—such as do-it-yourself home construction and repairs, food growing, household maintenance, parenting children and volunteering. In India such unpaid work can comprise up to 75 per cent of all production, particularly in agriculture sector.

Systems of National Accounts are based on GNP/GDP. Few economists, trade negotiators or development agencies questioned the basic assumption underlying it: that economies were generally in equilibrium, and that adding up a society's production and exchange of goods and services, measured in money terms, defined wealth and progress—however many social and environmental 'bads' came along with the 'goods'. Today's debates concern how best to calculate the costs of these 'bads' of production passed on to taxpayers or future generations. Some are easy to quantify: Costs of cleaning up pollution can be calculated, and their increase marches in lock-step with the expansion of pollution control and environment industry sectors.

***Confusing means with ends:*** Indian Government officials, business executives, academics and hundreds of thousands of civic organisations are beginning to agree that we have been confusing means (i.e. GNP growth) with ends (human development and the survival and further evolution of our species under drastically changed planetary conditions).

New environmental and resource realities, legislation and insurance liabilities are driving further overhauling of traditional accounts. There is a big issue over whether new indicators will be weighted in money terms to expand GDP, or whether the separate components—health, education, environment, etc.—should be 'unbundled' so that the public can follow their own concern and hold politicians accountable for results:

*Macro-economists* still try to expand GDP by pricing environmental amenities and costs. Social and natural scientists, while agreeing that environmental amenities must be valued at more than zero in GDP, advocate 'unbundled' physical indicators, such as water and air quality measures and rates of infant mortality. They suspect that economists 'contingent prices' for valuing the environment are theoretical and arbitrary.

Such 'Shadow prices' are derived by ecomomists from historic welfare theories and formulas based on 'willingness to pay' (WTP) of 'willingness to be compensated'. Thus, to arrive at a price for valuing a marshland (one of the most productive ecosystems on the planet), economists could poll voters and residents with no motives other than appreciation for marshes and their non-monetary or aesthetic values or their desire to preserve them and the rare species they might contain. Such contingent prices would be lower than those offered by a hotel developer with profit motives or by a biotechnology firm which had identified species in the area that could be used for pharmaceutical products. Worse, such pricing discounts poor people's needs and concerns, since they cannot afford to participate. Here the price system should be subordinated to more democratic decision-making, such as voting on whether or not to protect the marsh.

**Economic Accountability**

Most social and natural scientists, as well as voters, believe that economics must now take its place within interdisciplinary teams of statisticians from health, education, energy and environmental policy fields. Economics is not a science by rigorous standards, but a profession often lacking in the quality assurances and accountability that governs lawyers and doctors. GNP is a malfunctioning strand of our 'cultural DNA code'—carrying erroneous information and signalling to the body—politic a form of growth analogous to that of cancer cells which consume the host's body. The new national accounting methods being redesigned to correct or even replace GNP/GDP will function like healthy 'cultural DNA strands', newly spliced in to govern healthier growth and more normal development patterns for human societies. Quantitative growth is dominant as children grow to adulthood, but once their mature size and weight are reached, this gives way to qualitative growth: education, social skills, broader awareness and even greater ethical understanding and wisdom. The statistical shift from GNP/GDP to sustainable development indicators mirrors such maturing of societies, recognising new goals and the traits human beings must now rapidly develop if we are to restructure our society for sustainability.

The new scorecards allow Indians to move beyond economism and ideologies of left and right to measure results directly and hold our business and government leaders accountable for implementing progress on the major goals of individual voters, consumers and investors. The new scorecards can help broaden trade pacts to include sustainable development criteria.

# Bibliography

## Books


A.C. Pigou (1960). *The Economics of Welfare,* Macmillan & Co. Ltd., London.

Ahluwalia, Montek, S. (1985). *"Rural Poverty, Agricultural Production and Prices: A Re-Examination"* in John Mellor and Desai Gunvant, M. (eds.) "Agricultural Changes and Rural Poverty," The John Hopkins University Press, London.

Amartya Sen (1995). *The Hindu,* 6th November, Interviewed by Ramamanohar Reddy, Chennai.

Betellei, A. (2000). *Chronicles of Over Time,* Penguine Books, New Delhi.

Carr, Maryn *et al.,* (1997). *Speaking Out; Women's Economic Empowerment in South Asia,* Vikas Publications, New Delhi.

Chakravarty, Sukhamoy (1989), *Development Planning, The Indian Experience,* Oxford University Press, New Delhi.

Charsely, S.R. and G.K. Karanth (1998). *Challenging Untouchability. Dalit Initiative and Experience from Karnataka,* Sage Publications, New Delhi.

Chinnadurai, K. (1986). *Evaluation Study of Implementation of IRDP,* State Bank of India, Coimbatore.

Dantwala, M.L. (1996). *Dilemmas of Growth: The Indian Experience,* Sagar Publications, New Delhi.

Delige, R. (1999). *The Untouchables of India,* Berg, New York.

Desai, B.M. and N.V. Namboodiri (1993). *Rural Financial Institutions: Promotion and Performance,* Oxford and IBH Publishing Company Pvt. Ltd., New Delhi.

Dev, S. Mahendra (1999), *State Interventions and Women's Employment,* in T.S. Papola and Alakh N. Sharma (Eds.), *Gender and Employment in India,* Vikas Publishing House Pvt. Ltd., New Delhi, pp. 373-411.

Dharm Narain & Sen, A.K. *et al.* (1989), *Studies on Indian Agriculture,* Oxford University Press, New Delhi.

Frencine Fournier (1997), *Foreword, Poverty and Participation in Civil Society.* Edited by Yogesh Atal of Else Oyen, Abhinav Publications, New Delhi.

George Psacharopoulos and Moureen Woodhall (1986). *Education for Development: An Analysis of Investment Choices,* Oxford, New York.

Griffin (1979). *The Political Economy of Agrarian Change,* The MacMillan Press Ltd., London.

Griffin Keith (1978), *International Inequality and National Poverty.* The MacMillan Press Ltd., London.

Griffin Keith (1981). *Land Concentration and Rural Poverty,* The MacMillan Press Ltd., Hong Kong.

Gunnar Myrdal (1968). *Asian Drama—An Inquiry into Poverty of Nations,* Pantheon, New York.

Gunnar Myrdal (1970). *The Challenge of World Poverty: A World Anti-Poverty Programme in Outline,* Pantheon, New York.

Gupta, D. (2000). *Interrogating Caste: Understanding Hierarchy and Difference in Indian Society,* Penguine Books, New Delhi.

Haq, Mahabub Ul (1978). *The Poverty Curtain: Choices for the Third World,* Oxford University Press, Bombay.

Haq, Mahabub Ul (1997). *Human Development in South Asia,* Oxford University Press, New York.

Harper, M. (1998). *Profit for the Poor,* Oxford and IBH Publishing Co., Delhi.

Hirway Indira (1984). *Programmes for Poverty Eradication: A Critique of Target Group Approach,* Sardar Patel Institute for Economic and Social Research (Mimeo).

Holcombe, Susan (1995). *Managing to Empower: The Grameena Bank's Experience of Poverty Alleviation*, Oxford University Press, Dhaka.

IFMR (1984). *An Economic Assessment of Poverty Eradication and Rural Unemployment Alleviation Programme and their Prospects*, Madras.

Jackson Dudley (1972). *Poverty, MacMillan Studies in Economics*, MacMillan, London.

Karmakar, K.G. (1999). *Rural Credit and Self-Help Groups, Micro-Finance Needs and Concepts in India*. Sage Publications, New Delhi.

Kaushik Dasu (1984). *The Development Economy: A Critique of Contemporary Theory*. Oxford University Press, Delhi.

Khan Azizur Rahman and Eddy Lee (1984). *Poverty in Rural Asia*, Asian Employment Programme (ARTEP), Inernational Labour Organisation, Bangkok, Thailand.

Kuznets S. (1965). *Economic Growth and Structure*, Heinemann, London.

Lewis, A. (1966). *Development Planning*, Allen and Unwin, London.

Mahammad Haan Khan (1981). *Underdevelopment and Agrarian Structure in Pakistan*, A West View Replica Edition, West View Press, U.S.A.

Maheswari, S.R. (1985), *Rural Development in India*, Sage Publications, Delhi.

Minhas, R.S. (1974). *Planning and the Poor*, S. Chand and Company Limited, New Delhi.

Mukta Mittal (1995). *Women Power in India*, Anmol Publications Pvt. Ltd., New Delhi.

Myrdal Gunner (1968). *Asian Drama*, Volume III, Twentieth Century Fund, New York.

NABARD (1999). *Banking with the Poor: Financing Self-Help Groups*, CGM, NABARD, Hyderabad.

NABARD (1999-2000), *NABARD and Micro-Finance*, Mumbai.

Nanda, Y.C. (2000). *Role of Banks in Rural Development in the New Millennium*, National Bank for Agriculture and Rural Development, Mumbai.

NCERT (2000). *Human Development in South India*, Oxford, New Delhi.

Parthasarathy, G. (1982). *Integrated Rural Development Concepts, Theoretical Base and Contradiction, in Development Planning and Policy*, Edited by Gupta D.B., *et al.*, Wiley Eastern, New Delhi.

Rahman, Hossain Zillus (1998). *Poverty Issues in Bangladesh*, Power and Participation Research Centre, Mimeo.

Rai and Tandon (1999). *Voluntary Development Organisation and Socio-Economic Development*, Indian Economic Association, 82nd Conference Volume, Amritsar.

Sakuntala Narasimhan (1999). *Empowering Women, An Alternative for Strategy from Rural India*, Sage Publications, New Delhi.

Sen A.K. (1984). *Poverty and Famines: An Essay on Entitlement and Deprivation*, Oxford University Press, Delhi.

Shylendra, H.S. (1999), *Promoting Women's Self-Help Groups: Lessons from an Action Research Project of IRMA*, Anand, India, Working Paper No. 121.

The World Bank (2000-2001). *World Development Report*, Oxford, New York.

Todaro Michael, P. (1977). *Economics for a Developing World*, Longmans, London.

Todaro Michael, P. (1990). *Economics for a Developing World*, Second Edition, Longmans, New York.

Von Braun, J., Bayes, F. and Akhter, R. (1999). *Village Pay Phones and Poverty Reduction*. ZEF Discussion Papers on Development Policy No. 18, Centre for Development Research, University of Berlin.

Von Pischke, J.D. *et al.*, (1983). *Rural Financial Markets in Developing Countries: Their Use and Abuse*, John Hopkins University, Baltimore, U.S.A.

Yogesh Atal (1996). *Poverty and Participation of Civil Society,* Abhinav Publications, New Delhi.

Zeller, Manfred and Manohar Sharma (1998). *Rural Finance and Poverty Alleviation,* Food Policy Report, International Food Policy Research Institute, Washington DC, USA.

**Journals**

Amitava Mukherjee (1999). *Out of the Abysis. The Challenge Confronting Some Civil Society Actors,* Indian Economic Association, 82 Conference, Amritsar.

Awasthi, P.K., *et al.,* (1986). "IRDP: Receptivity and Reaction", *Indian Journal of Agricultural Economics,* Vol. 41, No. 4, October-December.

Bagchee, Sandeep (1987). "Poverty Alleviation Programmes in Seventh Plan: An Appraisal", *Economic and Political Weekly,* Vol. XXII, No. 4, January 24.

Bardhan, P.K. (1973). "On the Incidence of Poverty in Rural India of the Sixties", *Economic and Political Weekly,* Februry.

Bhat, Mazi, P.N., *et al.,* (1999). "Finding of National Family Health Survey Regional Analysis", *Economic and Political Weekly.* Vol. XXXIV, Nos. 42 and 43. Oct. 16-22/23-29.

Chambers, Robert (1994). "Poverty and Livelihoods Whose Reality Counts?" Overview Paper II, UNDP Stockholm Roundtable, Change: Social Conflict or Harmony? 22-24 July.

Copertake, James G. (1996). *The Resilience of IRDP: Reform and Perpetuation of an Indian Myth,* Development Policy Review, 14.

Dantwala, M.L. (1983). "Rural Development: Investment Without Organisation', *Economic and Political Weekly.*

Desai, A.R. (1987). "Rural Development and Human Rights in Independent India", *Economic and Political Weekly,* Vol. XXII, No. 31.

Desai, B.M. and J.W. Mellor (1993). "Institutional Finance for Agricultural Development: An Analytical Survey of Critical Issues", *Food Policy Review I, International Food Policy Research Institute,* Washington, DC, USA.

Ghosh, D.K. (1995), *"Group Cohesiveness in DWCRA Groups: An Application of Sociometric Approach"*, Kurukshetra, May-June.

Govil, R.K. (1982). "Micro-Level Planning and Rural Development", Kurukshetra.

Grewal, R.S. et al., (1985). "Impact of Integrated Rural Development Programme on Rural Women in Bhiwani District of Haryana", *Indian Journal of Agricultural Economics,* Vol. XL, No. 3, July-September.

Hara Gopal, G. & Balaramulu, Ch. "Poverty Alleviation Programmes: IRDP in an Andhra Pradesh District", *Economic and Political Weekly,* Vol. XXIV, Nos. 35 & 36, September 2-9.

Hirway Indira (1984). *Programmes for Poverty Eradication: A Critique of Target Group Approach,* Sardar Patel Institute for Economic and Social Research (Mimeo).

Jain, S.C. (1986). "Poverty Alleviation Programmes in India: Some Issues of Micro Policy", *Indian Journal of Agricultural Economics,* Vol. XLI, No. 3, Conference Number, July-September.

Karmakar, K.G. (1999). *Rural Credit and Self-Help Groups: Micro-Finance Needs and Concepts in India,* Sage Publications, New Delhi.

Kumar Rajinder, *et al.,* (1986). "Impact of Credit on Income, Employment and Capital Formulation of Rural Poor", *Indian Journal of Agricultural Economics,* Vol. 41, No. 4, October-December.

M.S. Kallur (2001). "Empowerment of Women Through NGOs: A Case Study of MYRADA Self-Help Groups", *Indian Journal of Agricultural Economics,* Vol. 56, No. 3.

Mosley, P. and R.P. Dahal (1985). "Lending to the Poorest: Early Lessons from the Small Farmers: Development Programme, Nepal", *Development Policy Review,* Vol. 3, No. 2.

NIRD (1985), "Employment and Income Generation Through IRDP, NREP and DRM", *Journal of Rural Development,* Vol. 4, No. 5, March-September.

Owusu, K. Opoku and William Tetteh (1982). "An Experiment in Agricultural Credit: The Small Farmer Group Lending Programme in Ghana", *Savings and Development,* Vol. I, No. 1.

Rajaram Das Gupta (2001). "Working and Impact of Rural Self-Help Groups and Other Forms of Micro Financing", *Indian Journal of Agricultural Economics,* Vol. 56, No. 3.

Rajasekhar, D., (1996), "Problems and Prospects of Group Lending in NGO Credit Programme in India", *Savings and Development,* Vol. 20, No. 1.

Sinha, S.P. and Prasad Jagadish (1980). 'Special Programmes for Weaker Sections: An Evaluation', *Indian Journal of Agricultural Economics,* Vol. XXXV, No. 4.

Stiglitz, J.E. (1990), "Paper Monitoring and Credit Markets", *The World Bank Economic Review,* Vol. 4, No. 3.

Thakur, D.S. (1977). "Rural Development in India: Past Experience and Tasks Ahead", *Indian Journal of Agricultural Economics,* Vol. XXXII, No. 3, July-September.

*The Hindu,* 11th May 2002, Chennai.

Yaron, J. (1992). *Successful Rural Finance Institutions,* World Bank Discussion Paper, 150, Washington, DC, USA.

**Reports**

Amitava Mukherjee (1999), *Out of the Abysis, The Challenge Confronting Some Civil Society Actors,* Indian Economic Association, 82 Conference, Amritsar.

APDPIP (2000), *On Andhra Pradesh District Poverty Initiatives Project Appraisal Document (PAD),* Report No. 20089, South Asia Regional Office.

Chief Planning Officer (2001). *Handbook of Statistics, Mahabubnagar* District, Mahabubnagar.

Chief Planning Officer Collectorate (2000). *Handbook of Statistics,* Krishna District, Machilipatnam.

Chief Planning Officer Collectorate (2001). *Handbook of Statistics,* Chittoor District, Chittoor.

CIRDAP (1998). *Increased Household Income and Rural Women in Asia, Impact on Status and Activities,* Dhaka, Bangladesh.

CIRDAP (1998). *Poverty Gender and Participation,* Dhaka.

CIRDAP (1999), *Rural Development Report, Centre on Integrated Rural Development for Asia and Pacific,* Dhaka.

CIRDAP (2000). *Poverty Gender and Participation,* Dhaka.

CMIE (2000). *Profile of Districts, Economic Intelligence Service,* October, Mumbai.

Government of Andhra Pradesh (1998). *Annual Report of the Commission of the Rural Development,* Hyderabad.

Government of Andhra Pradesh (1999). *Annual Report of the Commission of the Rural Development,* Hyderabad.

Government of Andhra Pradesh (1999). *New Series on State Domestic Product,* A.P., Hyderabad.

Government of Andhra Pradesh (2001). *Provisional Population Totals, Series 29,* Hyderabad.

Government of Andhra Pradesh (2001) *Statistical Abstract,* Hyderabad.

Government of Andhra Pradesh (2001). *Strategy Paper,* Hyderabad.

Government of India (1991). *Census of India,* New Delhi.

Government of India (1997-2002). *IX Five Year Plan,* New Delhi.

Government of India (2001). *Provisional Population Totals,* New Delhi.

Government of India (1974). *Towards Equality—Committee on the Status of Women in India.*

Government of India (1998-99). *Reports of the Commissioner of SC and STs,* New Delhi.

Haq, Mahbub Ul (1997). *Human Development in South Asia,* Oxford University Press, New York.

Holcombe, Susan (1995). *Managing to Empower, The Grameen Banks' Experience of Poverty Alleviation,* Oxford University Press, Dhaka.

IFAD (1996). *The State of World Poverty, Rome for a Discussion on the Process and Structural Causes of Poverty,* see Rovert Chambers (1983), *Rural Development, Putting the Last First,* London, Longmans, One of the Best Discussions on How These Perpetuate Poverty.

IFAD (2001). *Rural Poverty Report, The Challenge of Ending Rural Poverty,* Oxford, New York.

Indian Bank (2002-2003). *Annual Credit Plan,* Krishna District (A.P.), Vijayawada.

International Fund for Agricultural Development (IFAD) (1992). *The State World Rural Poverty—An Inquiry Into Its Causes and Consequences,* New York University Press, New York.

ISACPA (1992). *Independent South Asia Commission for Poverty Alleviation.*

NABARD (1999). *Annual Report,* Mumbai.

NABARD (2000). *Annual Report,* Mumbai.

NABARD (2001). *Annual Report,* Mumbai.

NIRD (1994). *Rural Development Report: Rural Employment,* Hyderabad, Andhra Pradesh.

NIRD (2001). *National Conference on SHG Movement in the Country and Swarnajayanti Gram Swarozgar Yojana (SGSY).* National Institute of Rural Development, Hyderabad.

PEO (1985). *Evaluation Report on Integrated Rural Development Programme,* New Delhi.

RBI (1984). *Implementation of Integrated Rural Development Programme—A Field Study.*

SAARC (1992). *The Independent Source Asian Commissions of the SAARC on Poverty Alleviation,* Dhaka.

South Asian Association for Regional Co-operation (SAARC) (1992). *Meeting the Challenge, Report of the Independent South Asian Commission on Poverty.*

The World Bank (1990). *World Development Report,* Oxford, New York.

The World Bank (1991). *Gender and Poverty in India*, Washington, DC.

The World Bank (1999-2000). *World Development Report 1999-2000*, Oxford University Press, New Delhi.

UNDP (1994). *Human Development Report,* Oxford, New York.

UNDP (1996). *Human Development Report,* Oxford, New York.

UNDP (1997). *Human Development Report,* Oxford, New York.

UNDP (2000). *Human Development Report,* Oxford, New York.

World Bank (1990). *World Development Report—Poverty,* Oxford University Press.

Yerramaraju, B. and Firdausi, A.A. (1995). *Evaluation of DWCRA in Prakasam District.* Sponsored by Government of Andhra Pradesh. Administrative Staff College of India, Hyderabad.

**Others**

Government of Andhra Pradesh, *Vision-2020,* Hyderabad.

Government of India (1985). *Five Year Plan Documents (The Seventh and Eighth Five Year Plans 1985-95),* New Delhi, The Planning Commission.

NABARD (1984). *Study of Implementation of IRDP (Mimeo),* Bombay.

Government of Andhra Pradesh (1999). *Vision-2020,* Hyderabad, India.

Government of Andhra Pradesh, *Guidelines for Swarnajayanti Gram Swarozgar Yojana, Panchayati Raj and Rural Development Department,* Hyderabad.

*IX^th^ Five Year Plan* (1997-2000).

*The Hindu* (2002). April 27, Chennai.

*The Hindu* (2002). Vision 2020.

# Index

## U



## W